The Merry Tongue

Dedicated to

all those who have lost a near and dear one.

© Noella Menon

2017 All Rights Reserved

The Merry Tongue

Author: Noella Menon

Title: The Merry Tongue

A Story of Love, Loss, Faith & Surrender

ISBN: 978-981-11-3303-9

Subjects: Faith, Surrender & Trust
Emotions
Spirituality
Christian Life
Women's issues
Devotional
Introspection & Reflection
Family Values
Marriage & Relationships
Love and Romance
Parenting
Widowhood, Loss and Bereavement
Relevant Biblical Quotes

No part of this book may be reproduced, transmitted or utilized in any form or by any means, electronic, or mechanical including photocopying, recording or by any information storage and retrieval system, without permission in writing from the publisher and author. All rights reserved.

Excerpts taken from *Streams in Desert - 366 Daily devotional readings* by L .B. Cowman Copyright © 1997 e-book edition edited by James Reimann. Use by permission of Zondervan. www.zondervan.com

The Merry Tongue

A Story of Love, Loss, Faith and Surrender

MILLY PEREIRA

❖ ❖ ❖

Written by

Noella Menon

Special Thanks
and
heartfelt gratitude
for their invaluable
contributions

To
Our Dearest

Albert, Roslynn
Satish, Preeti

and

to our most precious

Gia and Jade
Ved and Ronav

TO

GOD ALMIGHTY

OUR EVER LOVING FATHER

AND

TO

RONY PEREIRA - 1943-1988

A private edition of this book was presented as a surprise gift to Milly on her 70th Birthday. Her children jointly organised a family reunion for her on the 20th of February 2015 in Juhu, Mumbai. She is pictured here enjoying the serenity of yet another beautiful sunset.

"I read 'The Merry Tongue' in just a few hours. I feel this book has such a powerful message to share I couldn't put it down! It is simply BEAUTIFUL! It is a lesson for everyone of us and will surely be an inspiration for all women. I feel enriched." - **Dr. Armida Fernandez, Founder Trustee SNEHA & the Romila Palliative Care Centre (named after her only daughter who passed away after a long battle with cancer in 2015), Medical Director Holy Family Hospital, Mumbai, India.**

"When I am with Milly I feel rejuvenated and ready to face life's challenges. She radiates joy and her strength comes from 'Above'. We translated one of her testimonies taken from 'The Merry Tongue' to French and have shared it in our newsletter, with our F.O.L.O.R widows community here in France and other countries in Europe and Africa. Reading it makes it impossible not to believe that the Lord takes care of everyone of us. - **Alyette Vallette d'Osia, A French member representative of the F.O.L.O.R since 1978. She was widowed at the age of 29 years. Their sons were only 17 months and 2 months old.**

"The Lord said, "I will take the part of widows and orphans." 'The Merry Tongue' is a testimony to the promise of the Lord. Milly's children's' tribute in the book is a testament of the love, admiration and gratitude they feel for her. The book is a personal account of the loss and grief of losing a loved one. However, it goes beyond that. It is a deep spiritual surrender to the Lord who brings us out of the desolation of grief, widowhood and the difficulties of managing your life alone. The book is written in an engaging and easy narrative with beautiful sketches of family life. I personally feel the book reinforced my own experience with tragedy. I hope that 'The Merry Tongue' impacts many and helps to ease their lives into a new beginning of peace and renewal." - **Virginia Mendonça, School Teacher.**

Contents

Foreword	ix
Preface	xii
Prologue	xiv

FAITH FORMATIONS

Chapter 1: Home Is Where The Heart Is	1
Chapter 2: Ponytails And Braids	10

LOVE AND ROMANCE

Chapter 3: Soft Corners And A Few Rough Edges	23
Chapter 4: Teachers Treat	35
Chapter 5: A Rage Called Rony	44
Chapter 6: Hooked Line And Sinker	60

TRUST AND LEARNING

Chapter 7: Reality Bytes	72
Chapter 8: Parenting – An Art form	84
Chapter 9: Through Thick and Through Thin	121
Chapter 10: Turning Over A New Leaf	136
Chapter 11: Dreams Do Comes True	142

LOSS AND BEREAVEMENT

Chapter 12: Life's Unexpected Twists And Turns	148
Chapter 13: The Embrace Of Grace	153

SURRENDER AND GRACE

Chapter 14: Dealing With The Loss Of A Loved One	183
Chapter 15: Silver Linings Playback	191
Chapter 16: The Protector Of The Widow	203
Chapter 17: The Merry Tongue	211

Acknowledgements	231
About the Authors	232
Glossary	235
Bibliography	238

Foreword

Reading 'The Merry Tongue' has had a great impact on me. It is, in my humble opinion, a masterpiece of spirituality, containing many nuggets of gold that one needs to discover for oneself.

The book is unusually produced – the combined work of a mother, Milly Pereira and her daughter, Noella Menon. Noella was the recipient of her mother's narrations and a witness to her experiences over the years and has committed all this content to writing so beautifully. The book is a tribute as much to Noella as it is to Milly.

I came to know Milly during the time when I was closely involved with both our ecclesiastical movements for widows: The Fraternity of our Lady of the Resurrection (F.O.L.O.R) and the Hope and Life. Over the years, our acquaintanceship has grown. Milly joined both these movements and for a while even coordinated the F.O.L.O.R having being elected to its leadership.

The strength of the book is that it tells a very simple, homely, love story. I am sure most people would easily relate to the events narrated. As Milly faces the inevitable ups-and-downs of daily life, she slowly but surely develops a tremendous closeness to God. If she could cultivate such a communion with Him, so can all of us, but how is this to be done?

I found the answer in chapter 13, 'The Embrace of Grace', the day that Milly lost her husband. They were both young – in their early forties with three young children. She was distraught and shattered, feeling like she was going insane. At this precise moment, she heard the Lord say; "You said you trusted Me. Can you surrender?" And Milly did surrender!

It is after she surrendered to the Lord that her friendship with him started to deepen rapidly, through the trials and sufferings and paradoxically through the immense joys she experienced in her widowhood as well.

The Lord began to intervene in miraculous ways in her life. At every moment when she needed something, it was made available to her. Life took on a new efficacy. She shares in chapter 17, 'The Merry Tongue'; *"As everything keeps falling in place, wrongs become right, sadness flips to joy, weaknesses turn to strengths and as my destiny unfolds and beckons, as I live out each moment in faith, I truly internalise how much he LOVES me and mine and that reassuring knowledge in itself is like touching bliss!"*

Milly, who was once a shy, tongue-tied introvert received a prophecy at a prayer meeting, which foretold that her tongue would be used as a gentle council. As her life unfolded, her apostolate has indeed been more and more in the realm of words. She went on to complete a course in Counselling and has since been serving as a counsellor in a reputable school. She shares; *"I have slowly realised that, though I still feel nervous, the more I put my faith in Him and trust that he will take over my tongue, my thoughts and my actions, he has guided me with the wisdom to make a difference to the lives of many. All I have to do is lean on him like a crutch and His unrelenting support is, in fact, more like a prosthesis, which props me up, where I know I am too weak to stand on my own. I find that the butterflies leave my stomach and instead begin to fly forth in the rainbow! I find that my tongue is merry, my heart rejoices in the Lord and my soul is so grateful that I sometimes find myself "Bursting out of Love" to sing His praises!"*

All the fantastic gifts that she experienced, the graces and blessings that have come pouring into her life and her wonderful closeness with the *Living God* who intervenes in her life day after day and with whom she has developed an intimate rapport, are available to each and every one of us. All we have to do, like Milly, is learn to trust in and surrender our lives to Him. That is the message of this book.

Are you ready, dear reader, to TRUST in and SURRENDER to the Lord?

Bishop Bosco Penha
Em. Aux. Bishop, Archdiocese of Bombay

Initiator and Spiritual Director:
Fraternity of our Lady of the Resurrection (F.O.L.O.R)
'Hope and Life' Movement for widows since 1985
Small Christian Communities. (SCC)

Preface

These are reflections from the life of a simple Christian woman, brought up in post independent India; the intriguing land of paradoxes! Despite humble beginnings in an over-protected home, she meets her soul mate and goes on to nomadic and exciting times, travelling the world, experiencing her very own 'Happily ever After'! The sudden loss of her Prince Charming; the love of her life and the prop she completely depends on, turns her world upside down but she reaches out and truly finds her one and only true king - JESUS! She sees first-hand how God's promise to look after the widow and her fatherless children is true every step of the way. *His* unmistakable signs fill her with renewed hope. She gradually changes from a shy, introverted, tongue-tied caterpillar, living in the shadows of the significant others in her life, to a colourful butterfly with wings to fly. Freed from her cocoon she transforms into *'The Merry Tongue'*; allowing the Holy Spirit to work his wonders in and through her.

We are each like a beautiful and perfect instrument just waiting to be tuned. God waits to play his melodious masterpiece through us if we just allow ourselves to tune in. It will reinforce that to touch bliss even for a moment is to internalise that despite our weaknesses and inadequacies we are loved, treasured and accepted by God just as we are. The story shares nuggets that recount both happy and sorrowful times, will lend perspectives on family life, relationships, women's issues and discerning experiential thoughts on parenting with emotions and life lessons learned to imbibe or earnestly contemplate on.

It is our wish that anyone who reads this book will believe again that He works miracles even today and that His love can lift even the most sunken of us out of a deep pit and put a new song in our mouths, one that will sing praises to *His* name. We remain in awe of His Unfailing Love.

Prologue

"Mildred. I caused you to walk in the valley of Achor and I brought you out through a door of Hope; And you have walked well. I love you and you have my admiration. To the slightest touch of my spirit your heart has leapt up to respond. I say to you daughter, that if you will come and spend time with me, I will make you as Deborah was – A prophetess unto the house of God. You will be an arbiter in disputes. In you there is great unity in spirit and accord. They will call you to arbitrate in disputes and you will give wise counsel. You will be a healer of breaches where things are in discord. You will be actioned by my spirit. You will say things with a merry tongue; you are not one for graceless words and no one will take offence. I will cause you to instruct many and your words will carry because they are not your words but my words – living words passing from generation to generation even to those yet unborn. You will be a friend to many even when called to arbitrate and resolve disputes for your words will be graceful and yet alit with fire. You will not always meet with obedience; do not let it cause fear within you. Daughter, you have no idea of the life you carry with you. I trust you to walk in waterless places and there will be an oasis. Walk where there is no water and there will be flowers to bloom. You will not speak great things but simple things full of life and truth. My daughter Deborah was a prophetess close to my heart. My spirit will breathe into you the prophetic word from the heart of the Lord himself."

These words were written on a piece of paper and handed over to me while I sat in quiet reflection during our cell group meeting in 1989. Our prayer group leader, Doreen took it down as they were spoken by her friend Amalia, a deeply spiritual young woman, who had the gifts of the Holy Spirit: of knowledge, discernment and understanding, after years of meditation and prayer. It was a prophecy for me; a note of assurance. It was a divine blessing to proclaim that *His* work had already begun in my life and *He* was going to use me as *His* instrument.

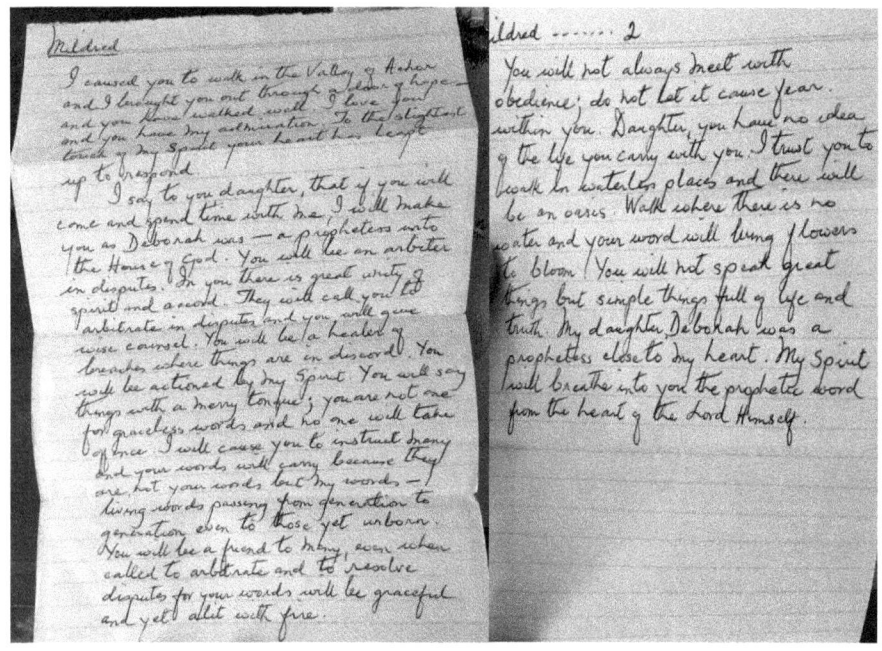

As I read the profound words and reflected on each sentence, the depth and weight of the words sunk deeper and were like a soothing balm for my soul; the gentle stroking of compassion, a firm enveloping of protection and a blanket of love, ensconced in His wisdom and fortitude; my conscious being could not understand wholly, but my soul connected, gratefully accepted and obeyed in faith.......

Chapter 1

Home Is Where The Heart Is

20th of February 1945 would be just another day in the history of humanity. Another child is added to the teeming millions in metropolitan Mumbai (Bombay as it was known then) in an over populated 'third world' country during the era of the freedom struggle, India's daunting fight against the British rule.

After much struggle, sacrifice and bloodshed in 1947, India finally became an Independent nation.

I was born to overjoyed parents thankful for their gift. The perspective was always that children were after all a gift from God and he would provide against all odds. It is to these faithful people, Amy and Valentine Pinto, that I was born. A bundle of joy as the old saying goes.

I was christened a week later - Mildred Piedade Pinto. I remember vividly my quaint little home, no more than 300 square feet. It was a one room, bathroom and kitchen apartment in an old building in 'Dhobi Talao'. We resided in Marine lines in south Bombay, India. The road I lived on was a narrow one-way street with hawkers on both sides, making it even more difficult to ride a bicycle, let alone a car into the lane. There was a hotel 'Vienna' opposite our home with a restaurant just below to add to the crowds during lunch hours.

We lived on the 2nd floor and to get to my apartment, we'd walk through dingy, dark stairways that would sometimes be home to a few rats and other rodents. Only the brave-hearted ventured up those wooden, creaky stairs when the sun went down. Nevertheless, in retrospect, this wasn't a big deal, because beyond those flights up was my home. A place I reckoned with, a place of security, comfort and a sense of belonging. So no matter how small a place, I loved coming back to it day after day.

It's the members of the family that make a home. My humble abode consisted of my parents and my elder brother who was four years older than me. He was tall and athletic. He took his height pretty early in life – He grew to be six feet tall with broad shoulders, a lean frame, high cheekbones and a chiselled nose, almost like a true artisan had had a hand in sculpting it. He had a perfect set of teeth and his smile lit up his handsome face. He loved the outdoor as much as my father hated it.

My dad was rather paranoid. He'd worry about every little thing. His fretting nature was probably the reason for his receding forehead with creases all across it. He had a long oval face and he seldom smiled. He could never bear the anxiety of us being out of the house too often or too late as his mind would simply lose all rationale. He could only think of the worst. He'd worry that we were injured, killed or lying in a gutter never to be found. No amount of my mother's attempts to calm his temper would make any difference whatsoever. Instead, he would give her a hard time in our mother tongue 'Konkani'. "It's entirely your fault", he would say. "You should be strict with the children". "Why don't you give them a deadline to come home by? I won't be able to forgive you if something happened to them."

I agreed, my father did tend to go overboard with the corrective action he took 'for our own good'. Back then, parents took the phrase, 'spare the rod and spoil the child' too literally and my father was no different. Eric, who being a boy's boy, climbed trees and the water tanks on the building terrace, played sports and ended up hurting himself more than a few times, was unfortunately the one who bore the brunt of that 'rod'. It was typical of my father to say, "No! Means No!" There was no question of arguing with him after that or trying to reason out with him. His word was final and his opinion was to be taken as God's truth.

It was little wonder then that my brother would do all it took to be outdoors. Probably the age gap and gender difference between us made him view me as too much of a little kid. He likes to remind me to this day, how he got into trouble with my parents on quite a few occasions because I tattle-tailed on him when he happened to annoy me or pull his 'big brother' pranks I didn't quite enjoy. I admired Eric. He has always been a person of great strength and character. I remember how he'd just stand there and take my father's scolding like an unshakable pillar.

My mother acted as the buffer in between. She'd try her level best to ease the situation but over time she realised that it was better to stay out of the battleground. I tried to somehow see beyond my father's nature – He loved us but just didn't know how to show it.

Maybe it was easier for me as I never really did experience his hot-headedness, probably because I was a girl, the baby of the family and mostly complied and conformed to his governance.

My father, Valentine, was a more outgoing personality unlike my mum, Amy (Eremit) who preferred the indoors. She was not much of a conversationalist. Her only true companion, with whom she confided, was my dad. He was a compounder by profession.

He loved politics and history. He'd read the entire newspaper from start to finish and be able to opine on almost every topic. He didn't believe in scrounging on healthy food. If one of us got sick, he knew exactly what to prescribe for us and he'd buy the medicine and take care of us till we got better.

First Holy Communion Dress made by my mum.

I remember this one time when I went cycling with my friends without his consent and had the misfortune of meeting with an accident. My bicycle went over a huge stone and I lost control of it and had a fall. I got a deep wound on my ankle. I recall crying more with the fear of how I was going to face my father, than with the pain. So I decided to hide it from him. When I came home, I quickly cleaned it in a way I saw fit. But one week later, I realised it was *far* from ok.

My wound became infected with pus. I could no longer hide it anymore. As soon as my father noticed me limping, the cat was out of the bag! He was furious that I hadn't informed him about it sooner. He was tempted to hit me in his anger. It was always his first reaction in such situations. But after he cooled down, he'd ensure that my mum tended to our wounds. He was actually a compassionate man although it wasn't immediately visible to most. He had single-handedly supported his entire family. He continued to support his brothers with their education even after he had a family of his own to look after and then later put them up and helped them to find jobs in Bombay, the city of dreams.

I loved my father and there was a definite connection between us. Just how deep a connection I was to discover many years later.

I was a quiet, reserved girl and liked the comfort of being around my mother all the time. She was my sense of security. Her firm reassurance and faith that God was watching over us at all times made me believe in His mighty power. Mum was so much shorter than Dad. She was hardly 5 feet 2 inches tall with blunt, straight hair that had already begun to have hints of grey at such an early age. She had a round face and a relatively wide nose. Her entire focus was to look after her family and their needs. She was simple but tasteful.

She'd keep aside money every month to buy material and would make the time to stitch the prettiest dresses for Sunday Mass or for special occasions like my first Holy Communion. I remember how angelic I felt in that flowing dress with pretty veil, designer candle and matching bag. She never went out much apart from going to bring the groceries or the 'bazaar' and didn't have many friends. She mostly kept to herself and her family and mixed with the neighbours only so as to maintain a good relationship with them.

I had grown accustomed to her presence in our home. She was

comforting, more understanding and very prayerful. It was her influence that begun my strong foundation in my Christian faith. She'd make it a practice to say the rosary in the evening with the entire family and she never missed her three-o-clock prayer. She taught us all the prayers and read stories from the Bible and insisted on us going for mass daily just like her.

My mother was always afraid of her own father. She never dared challenge his authority and kept a low profile, always doing what she was told. She wanted to become a secretary or do an office job but her father would not hear of it. She was educated in a British school in Rangoon, Burma and only much later did their entire family return to Goa to settle down.

My mother eventually became a schoolteacher and before she could actually start earning her own money or experience a little independence, she'd been 'packed off' to marry my father who was almost ten years older than her. She wasn't consulted. The proposal came in and they were grateful that the boy was so good that he didn't even ask for 'Dowry' – Yes surprising as it is, this social evil is still very much prevalent even today. Her father thought he was like a God send and reminded him of 'Joseph', mother Mary's husband.

In those days, 'Dowry' was an absolute must. The girl's father was expected to provide his daughter and her new family with money or gifts in kind. What started out to be a 'Kanyadhan', a beautiful tradition which meant gift of a daughter and 'Dowry' which was a gift from a girl's father to her, her inheritance if you may, turned out to be a 'must do'; a commercial tradition steeped in avarice and greed. To this day, we still hear horror stories of wives being beaten, harassed, tortured and even burnt alive because they did not give a satisfactory dowry at the time of marriage. The poor are known to borrow the money for their daughter's wedding and live in bonded labour for the rest of their lives to repay the loan with hefty interest rates to moneylenders or land owners.

So without further ado, my mother met her 'to be husband' and was married the following week and found herself on a ship to Bombay embarking on a journey with a stranger and a new life in a new city; Talk about the great plunge into the unknown! She was hurt that her parents decided all this in such a hurry without her consent and had virtually 'got rid' of her. Indian parents, feel morally obligated to settle their daughters well, into good families so that they can fulfil their duties. They feel a huge burden lift from their shoulders, knowing that they no longer bear the responsibility.

With my family in 'Zubeda Manzil'

To my mother's good fortune, her parents made a sound judgment when it came to selecting a good husband for her. My father taught my mother the vagaries of city life and was, in fact, the first to introduce her naïve mind to the 'birds-n-bees'. She was twenty-two at the time and was shocked at the very thought. She was given books to read so that she could 'educate' herself and grow up overnight. But aside from all that, my mother with her education and influence of the Irish nuns became a great companion to my father and he enjoyed discussing global affairs and politics with her as she had her own interesting perspectives to share.

My parents had their own set of beliefs and some of them were rigid, traditional and ritualistic. They were products of their past influences and they clung on to these 'value systems'. My father told my mother what to do and she obeyed. It was a natural transition for her. She did what she was told in her parents' home and did the same in her husband's home. She accepted her role and resigned herself to her purpose in life; Husband, children, cooking and cleaning had become her world and the reason for her existence. She was a devout churchgoer, prayerful and God-Fearing. I never knew our home without her. She was always there and I drew an unconscious comfort from that unchanging fact.

At some point in our lives, we ask ourselves the inevitable existential questions: "What is my purpose? Why am I here? Can I make a difference to the world?" We wonder if we'll ever find our true calling. Women play such a powerful role in the family. We create a balance, an equilibrium that keeps the home peaceful. Our inherent nurturing, tender, loving ways are like a nutrient rich soil in which our saplings take root. The deeper they reach inside this foundation, the firmer and stronger they become to reach out to the sun, to face the outside world with its strong winds, storms and sometimes incessant rain. We're like the unglorified mud; undervalued because we remain unseen but without which the plant will surely wither away. Our power to influence and shape a future generation is a purpose and calling in itself.

Good parenting is such an important responsibility yet none of us is ever formally taught how to become one. More than anything my parents ever told me or advised me, I imbibed their value systems by what I saw in them; how they lived, behaved and treated us and the people around them, with care and concern, respect, empathy and understanding.

It reminds me of an appropriate quote by the recently canonised saint Mother Theresa: *"What can you do to promote world peace? Go home and love your family."*

"Through skilful and Godly Wisdom is a house, a life, a home, a family, built, and by understanding it is established on a sound and good foundation, and by knowledge shall its chambers of every area be filled with all precious and pleasant riches - Proverbs 24:3-4

Chapter 2

Ponytails And Braids

I don't have very fond, everlasting memories of life as a student but there were a few episodes that did stand out. They made a difference to me because *I* had made a difference.

My school was not even five minutes walking distance from where I lived. 'Our Lady of Dolour's' was our parish and it had set up a school division.

My parents were advised to shift me to an all girls school. Our education came first to them so they were keen to do what was best for us. I was admitted to St. Anne's.

It was a huge transition for me. I can still visualize my mum speaking to the nuns on my behalf. It was here that I got my first dose of the glaring difference between the haves and the have-nots; I was made to feel it, let's just say. It was almost out of an Enid Blyton storybook; you know those typical schoolgirl books where you have the ringleaders, the troublemakers and the snooty making fun of the simpletons? Only this was reality and I was the scapegoat.

There was Josephine; full of life and very talkative, Fiona, Sharon and a few others who were undoubtedly the leaders of the pack. They all swooped down upon me like laughing hyenas; at least that's what they resembled in that particular nightmare of a first day in the new school. They began by opening my plain, brown cloth bag and sneering at how shabby it looked. They got hold of my pencil box, the one I'd been using for the last couple of years and they all simply burst into fits of laughter when they opened it.

In it lay an old-fashioned holder pen that was so out dated it needed to be dipped into an inkpot every now and then while writing. They all jeered and said, "Which century have you come from?" The fountain pen had recently become the rage and all of the other girls had got themselves, not only one but two of them. Here was I, a new girl with an old pen.

But as the old saying goes, I saw red. It was virtually like I was a latent bull in an arena of laughing spectators, being provoked beyond my limit. That was that! The last spear in my side. I was raging mad and without warning, I flared up and charged headlong into my opponents blindly with no rational thought. "Who do you think you are anyway?" I asked in a mighty powerful voice for a placid looking new girl on the block. "If I could afford a fancy pen like you, don't you think I'd have had one by now? I'm the new girl and I don't know anyone here. It's already hard enough for me and instead of making me feel welcome, you make fun of me? I'm disappointed. I expected more from the girls of St. Anne's."

And with that, I snatched the pen back, closed my bag and put it away from their prying eyes and although the tears were smarting my eyes, I refused to let them fall. The last thing I would do was show my vulnerability and weakness to these pack of…of… Well, there were numerous words that came to mind at that moment. I resented their superior attitude. I was always one to hold my own though, no matter what they thought of me. However meek and humble I appeared, I was a proud one at heart and would not allow them to get the better of me.

Retaliating in this vehement manner was a risk I had taken. After all, I would have to come back and mingle with these very girls for the next three years. They could have made my life a living hell, making it their business and past time to torment me, but low and behold, the exact opposite thing happened. They were taken aback and in their astonishment, they immediately backed off. One of them piped in from the back saying, "She's a fiery one, isn't she!? She's nothing like we thought she was." They all admired my nerve and began respecting me thereafter.

I became very friendly with a few and Josephine was later to become my sister-in-law. Life takes interesting turns when you least expect it. As the days past, I grew accustomed to my new school and opened up a bit.

I was in the ninth grade and you know how it is when you're that age, you're not only conscious of the way you look but more so, interested in how many humans from the opposite gender were taking notice as well; the girls in my class certainly were.

They all began wearing their socks low and their sashes alike just so they could look trendier in our drab uniforms. Some of them had begun growing their nails, shaping them and wearing stylish pins in

'Ivan and the Phantoms' – With the huge trophy the band won. Rony on the Extreme Left.

their hair, which was no longer tied neatly into plaits, braids and ponytails but was left as loose as was permitted. I, on the other hand, liked wearing my hair in a bob cut and I didn't bother with boys till a while later.

There was this young lad who lived in the neighbourhood. All the girls in my class were enamoured with him. He was tall and lanky with light grey-brown eyes and was attractive. To add to his popularity, he had a rock-n-roll band of his own called 'Ivan and The Phantoms'; Four members of which he was the lead vocalist. He had an excellent velvet voice and did a perfect imitation of the 'King of Rock', a rage in those days. 'Elvis Presley of Bombay' is what he came to be called. His band won an all Bombay contest for which they received a large trophy. The write up in the papers only increased his fan following and they all clamoured for his attention.

Those who knew him were proud to pair themselves with him and those who didn't would die for an 'intro'. Rony loved the attention, who wouldn't? One afternoon, when I was returning home from school with a friend, she offered to come out of her way to drop me off to my lane. No sooner had we approached the crossroads than a couple of guys approached us and began chatting up my friend like they were long lost pals. They all began making plans for a picnic and very casually asked me whether I would be able to make it. Without hesitation, I simply declared, "My mummy won't allow me, sorry! You all carry-on." Rony who seemed the most persistent of them all, offered to come speak to my mum for me, saying that we were all going to be in a huge group of boys and girls and would be back before sunset so there was nothing to worry about. I'd be in good company.
I didn't even consider it. I hurried home muttering apologies and later I

thought how rude and cold I must have come across. I was kicking myself for not acting cool and composed. Was my nervousness evident to them?.... to Rony? I thought he was a real decent boy and he looked kind of handsome too. Aaaargh! Why did I have to turn out like such a nutcase? I had spoilt such a nice opportunity to make friends with a heartthrob.

Anyway, that was that. There were no picnics, movies and outings for me. After all, I was too young, only in school and besides, when I asked my mother's opinion on how she felt about my going out in a group, she said, "There's a time and a place for everything. If there's this boy you like and if he's the one for you, he'll still be around when the time comes, don't you worry." So, I took her word for it and carried on my solitary life.

I had plenty of attention seeking souls in my class in school. It's interesting how you come across so many different personalities all trying to make their mark in the world. Some succeed and others don't. But in a classroom scenario, it's not very difficult to be outstanding. You can excel in academics or sports, extra-curricular, emerge as a leader or even become a ringleader; popular because of the amount of trouble you can cause and bring some naughty adventure into an otherwise dull routine. I particularly loved to read 'Mallory Towers'; novels that related stories about the lives of boarding school girls. Those paperbacks used to transport me to each and every adventure those characters experienced. It was so much fun. Something I would never do in reality was possible in an imaginary and fictitious world but there is nothing like witnessing a real live action scene, one that you're very much part of.

One fine Monday morning in spite of the sunny weather, many of us were experiencing those familiar Monday morning blues. To rub salt in our wounds our first lecture was Hindi language. I took a dislike to it even more because of the professor. He was ostentatious, loud and had the most high-pitched raspy voice. He had this nasty habit of repeating himself every now and then. Realising that there was a whole week ahead of us and we were made to endure the worst lecture first thing in the morning was sort of the sour icing on a rotten cake; a twist to that expression as it perfectly encapsulates the kind of mood that was floating around the classroom that day.

Mr. Singhal, the professor, walked in, in his usual eccentric manner. He was wearing a blue jacket on a yellow shirt with purple pants and that's not an exaggeration! His spotted tie was equally mismatched. He usually took the attendance first and he kept calling out roll numbers one by one until he reached number 42, Marion Martins. Instead of answering and confirming her presence, she took off on her own tangent. "What a lovely tie you've worn, sir!" She piped in. "I'm sure your wife picked it out for you. Was it a Valentine's gift? It's so you. It matches perfectly and really suits you." He began to blush with embarrassment. He muttered, "Keep quiet you! Sit down you!". Every sentence would annoyingly end with the '*you*' tag for some strange reason. The girls used to be in splits of laughter and the poor man could hardly bring order to the classroom. The time would fly and before you knew it, the class would be over and we'd be 'saved by the bell!' quite literally!

Mr. Singhal could not decide whether he liked Marion or hated her guts! She was the biggest troublemaker but at the same time paid him so many compliments. It was a difficult decision. One evening the decision was made for him. I think Marion went too far with the pranks. He walked in with a beautifully starched white shirt and she couldn't resist the temptation when her eyes fell upon her freshly filled ink pen on her desk. In that split second, she succumbed; ate the forbidden apple and there it was; a long streak of blue ink all across the back of his lovely, pristine, white shirt.

He, however, was blissfully unaware till he began to get suspicious with the snickering in the background. It seemed to get louder whenever he turned his back to the class to write on the board. He gave us a couple of quizzical looks but didn't really pinpoint what the problem was. Anyway, the bell rang and Mr. Singhal had to attend the next lecture in the adjoining classroom. As soon as he left our class, there was a virtual uproar as everyone burst out laughing. What was funnier was that hardly had our laughter died down when shrieks of giggles broke out next door.

One minute later Mr. Singhal stormed into our classroom waving a big ruler in his hand. He was close to hysterical. He ranted and raved and all of us took it with a pinch of salt till he came up with an ultimatum, much to our surprise and dismay. He demanded to know who had thrown the ink on his shirt or else he would detain us all from going home. With that, he stomped out of the classroom leaving us dumbfounded.

Everyone started to request Marion to own up to the incident but she was too scared. The pressure really began to mount when parents started to call and come to the school, hours later. Some of the girls wanted to go tell him the truth themselves if Marion didn't pull herself together. Finally, after much coaxing and cajoling, she resigned herself to her fate. She took me along for support and we both went to his office.

Marion didn't give herself the chance to back out. She walked straight into the room and began apologising profusely. "I did it sir, I was only testing the pen and the ink splashed on your shirt by mistake. I'm very sorry sir! Here let me take that shirt and get it laundered. That's the least I can do for this utter carelessness on my part." She actually reached forward to grab his shirt when he took a few steps backwards and yelled, "Stop it! Get out, you! Go!" and even though he was only talking to Marion, she took it to mean he had let us all go and said, "Thank you, Sir!" and ran back to tell everyone that they could go home. She was dreading the following day but the 'telling off' never really came. I guess he was a kind-hearted man after all and never held a grudge. This was confirmed when she actually passed her Hindi examination!

Each time I was faced with the prospect of writing this exam, I had butterflies in my stomach and I needed to visit the toilet more often than otherwise. Anyway, the examination day arrived and I, as usual, learnt the answers by heart without really understanding a word of it. I looked at the questions and began to write whatever I thought I knew. But I soon concluded that I wasn't prepared because for the most part, I was left staring blankly at the questions that had been re-framed to fool us fools who didn't know better.

Jennifer, one of my friends, must have noticed me looking into thin air and presumed, quite accurately, that I was blank. She impulsively decided to come to my aid. Before I knew it, I was staring at two papers; my own and hers! She'd swiftly and gallantly passed her answer paper on to me and I was left there aghast, scared, sweating…. but very tempted.

I knew it was wrong and I tried as far as possible to do what was right. But here was an answer sheet made available out of the blue. It lay there just waiting to be copied and to save me by the skin of my teeth. I succumbed to the temptation and began feverishly writing whatever I could. I reached the 6th line of the page when I saw from the corner of my eye, a white dress, just next to where I was sitting. I froze. It was the headmistress; a nun named Sister Anne; a fiery woman and a strict disciplinarian.

The chill hit my spine and I felt I couldn't move. Immobilised, I held my breath picturing her looking down at me holding another girl's paper in my hand. I didn't dare look around lest I gave myself away from the sweat on my brow and the fright in my eyes. Those two minutes seemed like an eternity but they did end and the nun went off to the next class on her supervisory rounds. I guess she was glancing around at the whole class and I, being just under her nose, was the least suspicious.

Phew! That was a close one. I literally wiped my forehead and was then faced with the temptation yet again. So instead of giving the paper back, half copied, I decide to go all the way. After all, the nun hadn't caught me red-handed. I was out of danger and I convinced myself to complete what I'd started. Imagine half the page written in perfect Hindi and the latter half of non-stop nonsense. I would surely be a sitting duck whose neck was there for the teachers ringing. I managed to pass that paper back discreetly and handed in my answer sheet. I felt sure I would pass but I wasn't very pleased with myself. I swore never to attempt to copy again in my whole life and I earnestly prayed that God would be merciful. I lived up to that vow too. I came out of the examination hall feeling weak in the knees. I buckled when Jennifer came up to me hurriedly and said. "I hope you didn't copy the 4th answer. It was a character sketch of my mother."

My heart sank. I couldn't rest in peace till the results, hoping against hope I hadn't been foolish enough to copy that answer. Everything was such a blur! I couldn't remember anything for the life of me. I hoped God had forgiven me and believed my vow to be honest. The papers and results were given out two weeks later and I wasn't caught. I passed the exam too. Thanks but no thanks to Jennifer, for sure!

Sometimes, we waver in our beliefs and principles and allow ourselves moments of weakness. But God is compassionate and forgiving and he allows us to falter so we may return to him; as long as we seek him out and truly ask for forgiveness with a humble heart, I feel he is ever willing to wipe our slates clean.

I wasn't too much into extra-curricular as well and I'd stick to the minimum that was expected out of me at school. I'd complete my class work, always did my homework on time and maintained my books neatly. Beyond the routine of going to school and back home, I didn't really venture further. However, in the 9th grade, the sports day was around the corner and all the girls in my division were taking part in some event or the other: whether it was athletics, the races, the pole vault, shot put, the javelin, gymnastics or the march past. They seemed to be contributing to their respective 'house' in some way. So, with a little goading from a few friends, I decided to put my name down for the 200 meters sprint. Besides, there was a rumour that the heartthrob of the area, Rony was going to show up at the event.

As I mentioned earlier, lots of girls had a crush on him and were very pleased to link their names to him. Ok, I'll admit, I too thought he was rather cool. So as the day approached, we all began preparing for the day. I had to get new sports shorts stitched and my ever so supportive mother helped with that. I couldn't afford to look shabby after all. I began drinking 'Complan', a health drink to boost my energy and stamina levels, something I lacked terribly.

There were many instances when I felt like backing out of the race especially when I learned who I was going to be competing with; the likes of Angie and Bertha, real speeders known to have secured several cups with illustrious school sports reputations over the years. But I believed in sticking to my commitments and seeing it through to the end. Besides, there were other incentives like er……Rony, to name one.

The day was finally upon us and as usual, I had butterflies in my stomach, an all too familiar phenomenon, I resigned myself to having to go through whenever there was a major event in my life. But somehow my seemingly timid nature never did stop me from diving into the unknown. "On your mark, get set, GO!" The race began and I could see Angie and Bertha take off like gusts of wind. One second there and the next, Poof! - Gone!

For the 1st hundred meters, I sprinted as fast as I could. I even managed to catch a glimpse of a group of boys in white, standing on the extreme left from the corner of my eye, one of whom, looked like Rony. Maybe it was a mirage. My mind was playing tricks on me because of my lack of concentration or merely the fact that my knees were beginning to buckle, as I didn't have the stamina enough to drive my legs to the finishing line.

My class teacher was standing on the side lines and I could see Viola close in on me on the left. We were both at this point contending for the 3rd place. To my surprise just when I was about to give into exhaustion, I could hear my teacher's distinct voice shout out, "Come on Mildred! You can do it!" That was all I needed; The encouragement spurred me on and gave me a new dose of stamina like manna from the heavens.

I mustered up every ounce of power I had and commanded my legs to quicken their pace. Viola, close on my heels started to fall back and a few seconds later, I touched the finishing line. I was ecstatic and received hearty congratulations from all my well wishers. This was my first award for sports. I felt like I would burst with joy when I was bestowed the honour of stepping up on the winning stand and was photographed along with my trophy; a small bronze cup.

I knew that I would treasure that cup for the rest of my living years. But that was not to be. When I returned home, trophy and certificate in hand, my parents were overjoyed and said. "You never fail to surprise us!" I liked that; the surprise element. It made everything that much more interesting and worth it. But unfortunately, an awful surprise was still to come. The following day, skipping happily into the drawing room, I discovered much to my dismay that the trophy was gone! Just like that!

I'd so sweetly placed it on the centre table in the middle of the room and it'd simply vanished! In those days, we were in the habit of leaving our doors open during the day and I wondered who had taken my one and only prize possession. It deprived me of my sole remembrance of my achievement in sports. I didn't have the photograph too and life was pretty depressing those next few weeks. It took me ages to get over the loss. It had meant so much. I convinced myself that no one could rob me of my memory. I decided to remember the joy and to forget the pain. To this date, I can relive the events of that race as vividly as if it were yesterday; the adrenaline rush, the elation, the glory, the pride et al. Life's smallest joys bring so much meaning to existence.

"Do not lay up for yourselves treasures on earth, where moth and rust destroy and where thieves break in and steal, but lay up for yourselves treasures in heaven, where neither moth nor rust destroys and where thieves do not break in and steal. For where your treasure is, there your heart will be also." - Matthew 6:19-21

Chapter 3

Soft Corners And a Few Rough Edges

Another memory I will never forget is my first experience of a missing heartbeat. I felt my heart shoot up to my mouth. There was a huge void in my chest and a surge of happiness in that split second of sweet pain. I know that almost everyone would have gone through a similar experience and would be able to relate to this utter thrill; that surge I liked to call the 'Zoom' feeling.

My teacher was congratulating me, when I heard a clear, deep voice behind me say, "Excuse me, Mildred." I swung around to see the face that belonged to that voice and low and behold, I was face to face with Rony! "Congratulations!", he continued. "You put up an excellent fight in the end." This was the moment I'd been secretly hoping for. I found myself staring blankly into his grey-brown eyes, only one step away from me. My heart leapt, skipped and jumped all at the same time.

It was indeed one of the most electrifying feelings but it also left me speechless. I don't even remember if I thanked him. I only know that there were no further words exchanged between us. I could have kicked myself for being so tongue-tied and aloof as if I couldn't have cared less. This was the second missed opportunity and somehow I felt there would be more to come. I felt sure that Rony had a soft corner for me. This tube light dawning was quite exhilarating.

I was, for the most part, practical and I lived very much in the present, day to day, moment to moment and I was mostly content with my life.

I had a loving home and that's all that mattered. It was simplistic. I spent time with my neighbours. We were one enthusiastic lot. Very often, we'd organise picnics, outings to the movies or the beach and building events where we'd either have enactments or simply a tea party that everyone would contribute to equally.

I had taken after my father, worrying about a lot of things. I didn't want to end up following in my father's footsteps and allowing these needless fears to get the better of me. I made a conscious effort to reign in my imagination. The last thing I wanted was for history to repeat itself where I ended up stopping my loved ones from experiencing the fabulous things life has to offer.

I didn't like hypocrisy and sometimes I found it would creep into my own actions. I tried my best to be up front and honest. I felt self-assured. I tried to be less bothered with what impression I might make or what others expected of me, though I have to admit it's easier said than done. I had become strong-willed and I knew my mind.

I was a regular at church and I didn't like to miss daily mass. The Eucharistic celebration and the church gave me a reassuring sense of peace. I was the quintessential 'God Fearing', pious, religious conformist. I wanted to do the right thing and be pleasing in His sight. I went to Sunday school, read the Bible, volunteered at church and actually felt like I was 'holier than thou' in many ways. I got "You'll make an excellent nun, Milly!" quite often. I wasn't sure if that was meant to be a compliment though and was a bit uncertain about how I felt about the prospect. I desired to do God's will alright, just like Mary had, but little did I know that just praying the rosary, saying "Alleluia!" and "Amen!" after lengthy prayer recitals didn't quite define a 'Holy' person in God's books - He had so much to teach me about really and truly knowing Him. I thought I was a devout Christian but I had no real spiritual relationship with Christ…as yet.

I know how I needed His favour during my tenth-grade examinations. How I got through was unbelievable; almost miraculous. I'd fallen very ill about four months before the board finals and I missed the preliminary exams due to this. I unfortunately contracted typhoid and would run a high temperature. My eyes were heavy and I couldn't focus on my books. In a minute or so my eyes would simply close and the print would blur. I'd begin to get a headache just trying to read one line at a time. It was a hopeless task and the teacher and principal advised that I sit for the papers later in October instead of attempting to do them and risk failure.

But somehow, I was determined to get it over with. I mustered up all the courage and will power I had in me and I managed to study enough to pass those examinations. I secured second class but was grateful that I had managed to get through the year. It was an achievement; one of my first major ones and I was proud of myself. Where there's a will, there's a way. The cliché was so true.

I had come to the end of a whole chapter in my life. I was finally out of school. It's a difficult stage because you're on the verge of a whole new beginning. It's the start of a new phase of independence, future career planning and the opposite sex. You're not a child anymore but neither are you a full-fledged adult. I always thought that adults, especially my parents had a very convenient double standard to deal with the 'terrible teens'. "Why you're just a child!" they'd exclaim, treating me like a little one while on the other hand, they expected me to do things independently; make my own choices, after all I was on the verge of adulthood and it was "high time I grew up and started acting like one." I was ready for 'The big bad world.'

I remember how relieved I felt to be out of school. I didn't want to see another textbook in my life. I decided that studying was definitely not my cup of tea. I told my mum that I intended to do something that didn't involve academics. I was exploring the idea of either taking up a course in shorthand or typing. Maybe I could get work in an office. My mother offered to find out what the options were. So I forgot all about it for a while. The summer holidays were on and I intended to enjoy it like anyone would after more than ten years of books, uniforms and rules. Yes! I was finally a free bird. It was now up to me to lift my wings and fly. I did just that. I took off to my homeland; The village of my ancestors and a paradise indeed.

Goa is so beautiful. It really is ideal for a holiday, with its picturesque beaches, small winding roads, quaint little cottages, coconut and mango trees, hammocks and friendly old people in their verandas. The weather was excellent although it would get quite hot in the afternoons. I went to live with my grandmother at our ancestral home and it was everything like I imagined it would be. The smell of Goan fish curry wafting through the air, cow dung floors and high ceilings, deep wells where fresh water was available and the mango, papaya and jack fruit trees in the backyard.

My grandmother on my mother's side was an intriguing old lady. Hortencia was her name. Apart from her physical appearance, I didn't feel the vast age gap between us, simply because she was so young at heart. She had a zest for life and an ability to empathise with all ages. I totally admired her for her broad-mindedness despite being brought up in a rigid environment, where the old school of thought prevailed. She had had a hard life. She was married off at the tender age of thirteen to a 'shippy', who was away at sea for the most part of the year and was made to stay at her in-laws home where she didn't feel comfortable.

My grandmother went through a tough time when my grandfather lost his entire life savings in embezzlement and the family had been forced to migrate from Rangoon, Burma back to her homeland Goa, where they eventually built back their lives. She emerged stronger for it and had gained life lessons from these adversities. She was indeed a pillar of strength that looked only at the positive aspects of life. She understood that trials and tribulations are all temporary phases of life that everyone has to go through to become stronger and value the good in their lives.

She had put on a lot of weight since I last saw her but she was still energetic and refused to have me spend lazy hours at home. She felt that a young girl like myself should be going out and having a great deal of fun. She would encourage.... No!...make that prod me into hiring a cycle and taking it for a ride in the countryside. She arranged for the neighbours to take me out and show me the lovely sights of Goa. All the youth of the village used to arrange a bus and take off to the beach, which was a twenty minutes drive from where we lived. We'd play games on the beach, go for a dip, and take long strolls and it was a lot of fun.

My grandmother used to try and pair me up with some nice boys in the neighbourhood but I wasn't interested in that kind of thing. I loved lazing about actually. After lunch, I would take up a novel and read till

I dozed off. It was the simple things I enjoyed the most. The food was excellent as well and I relished the Goan curries and typical Goa rice; thick, grainy, puffy and delicious. I relished 'Balchaon'; a Goan speciality pickle made of salted prawns, spices and vinegar. I pigged out on Goan sausages specially prepared at home, made of meat and marinated in pungent spices and dried in the sun for several days till the meat absorbed every little bit of the spices and tasted heavenly. I put on a few kilos with all the gorging and idling I did.

I loved the holiday and really appreciated my grandma's efforts to entertain me with her humour and stories of the past. She used to give me sound advice and I admired her deeply for the way she continued to live and manage things self-sufficiently, all alone, never once grumbling about the hardships or moaning the loss of her husband. I thought about how I'd like to become just like her when I grew old; independent and so full of life right to the end.

Glad to be a college girl

I'd often ask my grandma if she wasn't scared. What if she fell and there was no one around to help her? Wouldn't she rather come live with us in Bombay? She just smiled and said, "What's there to be scared about when God is there? If I fall, then he will send someone at that moment to help me and if it's my time to go then I'll go."

I thought about what it was to be happy and live a meaningful life. I admired people who were completely at ease with themselves, knowing their strengths and weaknesses and were comfortable in their own skin no matter what the world thought. I began realising that all of us are children at heart. I thought about how we're only conditioned to behave in an appropriate manner in public and how it was a pity that a lot of us land up doing what is expected of us rather than what we really want to do. I tried hard not to have high-handed, impractical expectations and I absolutely loved being self-sufficient. I guess my grandmother had a strong influence on me.

I returned to Bombay after about a month and a half. I had the healthy suntan glow, evidence enough that I had enjoyed myself to the fullest. My mum at once began questioning me about my next plans. She was concerned about what I should take up as a career. She was aware that I had expressed a desire to take up a job but was not keen that I end up in a typical office set up, although she had always admitted to having a similar desire when she was young; to become a corporate executive. Her elders were dead against it because the inevitable always happened; "office girls land up in their bosses' laps" she would repeat what she was told. Her motherly instinct related to this more than ever before. So she did some spadework and found out about an interesting relatively new line of education, specially designed for women who wanted creative careers. She had heard that it inculcated good feminine qualities and helped women even if she chose to be a homemaker.

Mums do so much to keep the family together in every respect. My mum did her best too and though when we're young we take her influence and guidance for granted, we realise just how much our mothers do for our emotional well-being only a full circle later when we become mothers ourselves.

Things weren't always hunky dory though and I got to experience first hand this important role a mother plays in her family when my mother took ill one day. It was one tough phase; one I preferred not to speak of much. My mother had suddenly started behaving strangely. She'd mutter under her breath and began to become suspicious of everyone around. She spoke of people plotting against her. We had taken her to a doctor who recommended we see a Psychiatrist. They felt she might be showing signs of schizophrenia.

My dad wasn't convinced and neither were we! She was perfectly normal the day before. Something was wrong but we weren't quite sure it was mental illness. We were in denial; It was too sudden. We took her to several doctors for second and third opinions and I remember how we kept praying we were able to get an accurate diagnosis. That time was such an emotional roller coaster for all of us. My dad would lose his patience and we didn't know how to reassure mum that no one was plotting against her or out to hurt our family. I took over managing the household in whatever way I could. She wasn't able to function normally.

Finally, after several months, the 4th doctor we took her to said it might be because of her thyroid levels. He recommended we do some tests and it turned out to be a deficiency. He prescribed a pill to regulate the production of the hormone and it worked wonders! She was back to normal again within an hour of taking her thyroid medicine; just like that! It was a chemical imbalance all along that was causing her to hallucinate. Shows how little we know of the body, the brain and its functioning. Praise God that we were led to do the right thing at the right time and we had our mother back, literally! Life certainly threw a googly our way more than a few times but we got through it with God's grace and our family bonding grew stronger because of it. I learnt a few things about my own resilience and capability like never before. One thing's for sure, I valued the presence of my mum and began to take her for granted less.

So, in the mean while I had applied for the 'Home Science' diploma course for two years at Nirmala Niketan an institution strictly for women only, opened and run very efficiently by nuns. I remember them having given me a scholarship as I was unable to afford the hefty term fees. I do believe that God looks after our every need. He provides against all odds.

I was instructed to buy the course material and was given the syllabus. I got a rude shock. There I was, having joined a diploma that was supposedly going to help me develop my domestic and culinary skills and what I saw staring at me in the face, were heavy textbooks with brain taxing subjects: Psychology, Physiology, Chemistry, Biology, English literature, Gynaecology and Obstetrics, Nutrition and the extracurricular like needle-work, culinary classes etc. So much for not wanting to look at another study book in my life.

I reconciled myself to two years more of rigorous study and as we got deeper into the topics, I found them pretty interesting. I had to submit journals and do extensive research in the library and laboratory.

Compiling information, presentations and deadlines became the norm. I enjoyed learning how to make stuffed toys. We mad a teddy bear and it turned out so well. It was so durable that it lasted for many years. One of the few mementoes I preserved and cherished.

I learned how to stitch my own clothes and had so much fun sewing trousers, slacks and dresses with interesting colours. I began to look trendy in my creations and eventually I thanked my mother for enrolling me. It was an all round education. I fared well in the academic subjects and the nuns had taken a special liking to me.

There was this exhibition organised in the college. It was like an open event where other colleges including parents came to see the exhibits put up by the students.

They had organised a fashion show in the evening with lights and a long ramp. I was quite excited to have been chosen as one of the models. I had shoulder-length, wavy black hair and looked rather nice in the outfits we were given to showcase; all designed by the fashion designer students. What a feeling that was! The grandeur of walking in stilettos, chin up, with a stern but sophisticated look. We had to walk elegantly to the tunes and beats of the music in rhythm. I felt nervous but elated while walking down that ramp, hearing catcalls from among the audience. I felt so blessed to have had this opportunity most girls usually only dreamt about. I certainly felt special that day. It was a lovely experience - One I shall never forget.

Graduation day with our certificates in hand – beaming from ear to ear!

On completion of the two years, I graduated and the nuns made me an offer I couldn't believe. They were willing to send me to Madras (now known as Chennai) for further studies where I could get my degree in Home Science along with a part time job training younger students. They told me that I would be looked after; boarding, lodging and food. I'd be paid a stipend to get by. It seemed too good to be true. It was an opportunity to be independent. My parents would not have to spend towards my education anymore. It would be an exciting experience like an adventure. I'd get to see another city and be able to fend for myself. I knew it would do wonders for my self confidence.

With my students and the teddy bear soft toy we had made in class

I had worked out all the pros and cons in my mind and the pros seemed to far outweigh the cons. I decided that I would take it up and proceeded to inform my parents about the proposition and my decision. My father just sat there and listened to me ramble on about how exciting it was and how I'd benefit in every way. He didn't say a word nor did he react throughout my elaborate explanations.

After I had said what I had to say and looked to my parents for approval, he just sat up in his armchair, looked me straight in the eye and in a low and very flat tone said; "We don't want!" That was that. My destiny had been decided for me. My father's word was always final. There was no question of arguing or seeking explanations from him. Even my mother was against the idea so there was no hope of getting her to act as my ally. For her, it was more the unbearable idea of my having to live separately, away from home for so many years. So, she wholeheartedly supported my father's decision and nothing I could say or do would convince them otherwise. I felt I would be giving up a once in a lifetime opportunity and I would regret it for the rest of my life. It would always be a case of 'What if' later on.

Anyhow, I was never one to disobey my parents. The nuns were very disappointed when I told them and very sweetly offered to come over to speak to my parents but I declined and thought of what I could do next. On their advice, I took up the teacher's training course and I began teaching immediately at Nirmala Niketan itself. It was strange having to relate to girls nearly my own age, as their teacher. I took the needlework classes and I enjoyed imparting my practical knowledge on stuffed toys, slacks etc. to them. I became fast friends with most of the girls. The teacher's training course was great fun too. We had to take various subjects as part of the practical training. We were assigned points and were appraised on different parameters. I had turned a different corner but I still found my way.

"For I know the plans I have for you, declares the Lord, plans to prosper you and not to harm you, plans to give you hope and a future."
- Jeremiah 29:11

Chapter 4

Teachers Treat

After I got my certificate to teach as a School Teacher, I heard there were immediate openings at St. Anne's girl's high school. They required a class teacher.

With a colleague at a picnic!

I was now a member of the faculty and had to mingle with the very teachers who had taught me a few years ago. Some of the senior teachers were still there and they were very nice to me. They made me feel welcome and comfortable. I soon made friends of my own. You quickly learn the politics and protocol in the staff room.

I was doing reasonably well at St. Anne's high school but didn't feel a sense of fulfilment. For one I had been shifted from taking English and Science to needlework, which was fast losing its novelty and secondly I was restless for change.

Eric came up to me one day and told me that he had heard that there were openings at St. Xavier's High school. A very reputable school, run by the Jesuit priests known for their high standards in education. So I made out my application and called the school for an appointment with the principal, Fr. Hillary Miranda.

I was nervous before the interview. My palms had begun to sweat and it wasn't even warm. I always said a prayer before a new venture asking or rather begging for peace and calm and that all should go as planned. I was finally called into his office.

I forced myself to smile but it soon turned into a genuine one because Fr. Hillary was so warm and sincere.

He called me in what seemed to be one of the most soothing and comforting voices I had heard. It was husky yet so gentle. "Mildred! Come! Come! Have a seat." He said. "I can already feel that you are going to be a great asset to this school. It was something about his positive attitude or warm, genuine demeanour that made me find my voice again. We chatted informally for a few minutes after that and I found myself completely at ease as if I was talking to a close confidante.

Fr. Hillary Miranda made an instant impact on me; a strong, powerful impression that only grew better and better as the years went by. He was a remarkable man; A man of deep faith and understanding. He was to become one of the most influential people in my life. I'd call him my spiritual mentor; one of the few people who truly knew the meaning of life. Only a man of God could have been so open-minded at such a young age. Ever since I can remember, I knew Fr. Hillary to have been calm, peaceful, and comfortable with him self and others; a father figure in more ways than one to most. He had a unique gift of making everyone he met feel special. I always felt that we shared an extraordinary relationship and that he truly valued our friendship till I realised, many years later, that practically everyone he was close to felt the same way.

How brilliant to be able to make a difference; To be able to touch people's hearts and make a change through love, concern and understanding. Great is the one who is able to command respect rather than demand it. Fr. Hillary Miranda was such a man who you couldn't help admire. His opinion meant a great deal to people he was close to. His friendship was treasured and his guidance was revered.

Psychiatrists say that you have an average of five significant or pivotal role models in your life that shape your personality or could perhaps have changed your life for the better or for the worse. I am certain that Fr. Hillary would be that 'significant other' in the lives of all those who had the good fortune of knowing him.

The job was mine and I was requested to start on the following Monday. So there, you have it; new beginnings, finally a break in the monotony and the stagnation. I was ready to make a fresh start and for once, apprehension didn't get the better of me. I felt rejuvenated and excited to be part of a recognised and admired institution.

I was assigned to the primary section to the 1st and 2nd standard boys. They were really cute but a hand-full all the same.

The teachers were more on my wavelength. They were fun loving and humorous. We'd share classroom quirks during the break and laugh at the silliest of things. We'd wait for the delicious snacks that were offered to teachers on the house, courtesy the principal on special days and birthdays. There was nothing like hot tea to quench that thirst and to give us a new lease to carry on for the rest of the demanding day.

On holidays or after school we'd plan to go to the theatre and watch the latest movie in town.

We'd make sure to save up a little money to go out for lunch to a recommended restaurant. I particularly liked eating roadside fast food. I loved 'Pani Puri', 'Bhel', 'Sev Puri', 'Dahi Batata Puri' or the hot and spicy 'Ragda Pattice'.

The Parsi Dairy farm outlet was indeed a treat located on Princess Street, it served the most delicious 'missal', my personal favourite in addition to its 'Lassi', 'Pedas' and other delectable sweets. A good 'Desi' Chinese meal was my other weakness. It felt so good to be earning my own money and to be able to do with it what I pleased with no questions asked. I simply enjoyed every day and looked forward to going to school. It

Outing with a few teachers

was the spirit of freedom and independence that was most exhilarating. Those were some of the best years for me.

I was lucky to have joined the school at the right time too, for it was to be the centenary year of St. Xavier's High school. Hundred years was no small feat. The entire year was dedicated to festivities and celebrations and a splendid build-up to the main event to commemorate the opening of the school. I recall how we teachers were given the overall responsibility to plan all the events for the year and to make sure that the celebrations were spectacular. Initially, we had formed a committee and we decided to get the PTA involved too.

Some of the other celebrations included a fully paid trip for the teachers and selected students to Delhi and Agra. I was so excited to be given the opportunity to make my first trip out of Bombay. We went by train and the journey was long; more than 24 hours, but it was an exciting and thrilling experience.

At the Taj Mahal, Agra

You are virtually transported to the mystical land of the Moghuls in the form of the 'Taj Mahal' in Agra, a surreal place a few hundred kilometres from New Delhi. It is a spectacular monument with the most intricate carvings I had ever seen. The place has an ethereal aura as if it's an illusion.

We took some memorable photographs of us standing at the helm with our sunglasses and scarves. The students, who could afford the trip, thoroughly enjoyed their excursion. It made a world of difference to their newfound interest in Indian history. Something the plain old textbooks weren't able to achieve through their non-descript narratives.

Teaching in St. Xavier's was most enjoyable. I'd look forward to a new day at school. Every day had a story to tell. I remember how I'd try to put to practical use my acquired knowledge of textbook child psychology, to try and figure out the best way to handle different boys according to their personality types.

'Farhad' for example was a rather timid little fellow who just refused to answer any questions in public. I realised that he just needed time and space and a whole lot of encouragement to come out of his shell.

Class Photograph with my students at St. Xavier's School, Mumbai

He'd creep up behind me after the bell had gone and would gently tug at my skirt, saying, "I know the answer to that question you asked, teacher. Can I tell you now?" He was actually a bright boy but on some further investigation, I came to know more about his background. His parents were extremely protective over him. His mother was strict and didn't allow him to go out much and mix with the other children for fear that he might get hurt while playing. He was her only child after a painful pregnancy and she was paranoid that he might be too weak to take too much of outdoor exertion.

I asked to speak with both his parents to help them with their anxiety. They began to realise that their over cautiousness was affecting the development of their son and that if they didn't loosen the apron strings a tad bit, he'd be likely to turn into a 'mama's boy' and this could hamper his inherent talents in the long run.

After months of conscious effort on their part, Farhad started becoming more vocal, assertive and began taking an active part. His academics took an upturn too, much to the delight of his loving parents. His mother was grateful and shared that it was difficult to ease up. She admitted that she'd worry about every little thing and this anxiety overruled her better judgment. She tended to dote on Farhad, perhaps smothering him which was stifling her child's growth.

Another story, a personal favourite, was about Craig, who was labelled, the 'naughtiest' boy in the class. He was a bundle of energy and keeping him in one place was next to impossible. He'd create chaos almost every second of the day with his jabber, his laughter or his pranks. He would throw rubber pieces on the other boys and wouldn't spare the teachers too. He'd scribble on the covers of other student's books and make paper rockets that he'd throw from the classroom window. He would never seem to know the correct answer to any question but that wouldn't stop him from answering anyway.

He'd concoct a story of his own with no relevance to the question asked and waste precious time. He was always dirty and unkempt with his shirt hanging out and laces open. He'd have a scruffy face with black sticky dirt all over his mouth and nose. Even while the lesson was in session, he'd empty someone's textbooks on the floor and create some kind of commotion or the other. No amount of correction, scolding or remarks in his calendar seemed to have any impact on him whatsoever.

One day, I suddenly realised that he was smiling from ear to ear while I was scolding him for eating a poor boy's snacks from his tiffin box. The more I raised my volume, the happier he seemed.

He'd simply do anything to get my attention, even if it meant my disapproval. I discussed the situation with the other teachers who all agreed that we needed to speak to the boy's parents. I was saddened to learn that they were going through a separation and his mother had taken up a full-time job to earn a living to support her family.

She hardly spent any time at home and Craig was left with her own mum for the most part of the day. She said that he started throwing temper tantrums and would not eat properly. He didn't want her to touch him when she returned home from work and he would shout and scream at his grandmother, throw his toys all over the place and create havoc.

She was disturbed by his uncontrollable behaviour but didn't know how to handle the problem. I instinctively felt, that the only way to get through to him was an overdose of love and care. I requested his mother to start treating him with all the love and tenderness she could possibly give him. I told her that it would be ideal if she could perhaps give up her full time job and take up a part time assignment till he gets adjusted to the idea of his father not being around anymore.

If she could spend all her time showing him how much she cared for him that would really help him heal. She agreed that her divorce counsellor had also told her that very often children of divorced or separated parents cannot deal with the stress of understanding why their dad doesn't come home anymore or why he doesn't call. They feel like it is their fault and that their parents don't love them anymore. They often get torn between the two and feel caught in the middle. Tears came to her eyes. She promised that she would do everything it took to get him to change. At school, all the teachers changed their way of handling him. Instead of shouting or punishing him, we'd patiently explain what we expected of him each time.

Myra, his mother, we learned had given up her full-time job, spoken to the boy's father and they had reached an agreement that he would spend time with his son as often as he could. He had also promised to pay a monthly alimony for their welfare. It took months before Craig began responding to our 'treatment'. But the biggest joy was when he started showing signs of settling down. His hyper activity eventually diminished a great deal and his grades improved. His turn for the better and the affection he began showing was perhaps one of the great satisfactions I felt as a teacher. We teachers were paid minuscule salaries as compared to other professions. In retrospect, though it seemed like a pittance, it was a fulfilment like this that made our efforts all worthwhile. What a noble profession teaching really is! How gratifying it was to make a difference and mould a little life!

"Let my teaching fall like rain and my words descend like dew, like showers on new grass, like abundant rain on tender plants." - Deuteronomy 32:2

Chapter 5

A Rage called Rony

One day the postman arrived with two envelopes addressed to me. I was thrilled. It was always so exciting to find out who had sent you a letter. I hastened to open it and much to my surprise and secret delight, I found a card. The first one was a hand painted picture of a big black ship with a red border. It was sailing on blue waters with a vast blue expanse of sky above. Inside the card, it simply read, "Thinking of you. Thought you'd like to see what kind of a ship I'm sailing on right now." It was signed "From Rony". I was over the moon. I couldn't help go around with a glazed look in my eyes and a plastered smile on my face the whole day after that. He was actually thinking of me!

He remembered my name and my address and wanted to make sure he was in the picture. How right he was! I had thought of him quite often and what it would be like to bump into him on my way to

Rony on board his ship.

church perhaps. But there had been no sign of him for a very long time and I had almost given up that girly dream for good. So, he had been away at sea all this time. No wonder I hadn't seen him for so long. He didn't mention when he was due to come back. I felt light-headed and longed for his return, storing away the card in a very safe and treasured place.

Rony with his Dufferin mates (Extreme Left)

My home was walking distance from the school. It usually took me a leisurely 15 minutes to get from Metro to Sonapur. One evening as I emerged from the school gates glancing at my watch, I spotted a familiar face, a face that made my heart flutter just a wee bit. It was a lean face with a well-defined jaw line, an adorable but rather deep cleft in the middle of the chin, a large nose, and lips that creased into an absolutely delightful smile. His teeth weren't exactly perfect but that one tooth overlapping the other gave him added character. His skin was tanned and his eyes were the highlight of his handsome. He was too good-looking to be trusted was my presumption. The last thing I would betray was that I was also one of those many girls that had fallen for his looks. So I made a special effort to be discreet and hold my reserve at all times.

Rony strode up to me smiling his charming smile and talking his charming talk. I saw him almost in slow motion. His lips were moving, his eyes gleaming but I didn't seem to hear his words. "……..so I'm glad I got you before you left." He was saying. "I just got back from an eight-month stint. It feels good to be back in Bombay, at home." Do you mind if I walk with you?" and before I could answer he was by my side carrying on his chatter. "I've been meaning to get in touch with you for some time now. I met Judith who told me that you get off from school at 4.00 pm so I thought it would be the perfect opportunity to meet you. If you're not in a hurry, would you like to get a small bite and some coffee or something? I know the perfect little place. You'll love it." I don't remember answering or consenting. All I could remember was walking down with Rony in the direction of 'Blue Star' – a restaurant I had only heard of but never sampled. I found myself seated opposite him in the quaint café, munching on some delicious treats and sipping hot tea – I was having what seemed to be my first ever date – Totally impromptu!

The unplanned… The unexpected. Ah! Always the most fun. I hit it off with Rony. We gelled well as he was a non-stop talker…simply loved a good listening ear and I was just that; the world's best listener. I was all ears and found his sea-faring tales of far away places quite enthralling.

He told me about the hard life he had had as a 'Dufferin' cadet. How the seniors like the 2nd, 3rd and 4th officers would make him and his batch mates do all the dirty work. Scrubbing the galley and the deck, cleaning the toilets were just a few of his menial tasks. It was a customary ritual, apparently, to fling shoes at the cadets. The officers gave them a deadline by which all the dirt was to be removed and the polish had better shine on their shoes or else they'd get them flung at their heads the next time.

He related how he had some close friends, one of whom was Rusty, a Parsi lad who he grew very close to over the years. Rusty was from a well to do and aristocratic family in South Bombay. He had inherited his family business – Photography. They had their own studios. However, Rusty wished to become a self-made man and wanted to do something different. He was one of the most hardworking and dedicated people Rony had come across and most importantly an excellent human being.

An Officer and a Gentleman - Rony with his best friend –Dufferin Cadets.

He was generous and warm-hearted and thought the best of people. Rony told me how he had learned a lot from Rusty. They helped each other a lot and Rony could not forget how Rusty would play his surrogate father at 'Dufferin'. He would help to have his uniforms washed and ironed for him, polish his shoes and ensure that Rony woke up on time in the mornings to report for duty. I just sat there in silence. At the most, I responded in monosyllables or pretended to be sipping my tea most of the time. But I enjoyed myself thoroughly. Rony was as spontaneous as I was inhibited, as talkative as I was mute, was as captivating, as I was dull but how I wished he would go on and that date would never end.

I was hoping against hope that he'd mistake my reserve and silence for subtle intelligence and be mystified with what could easily be mistaken as my lack of enthusiasm.

Guess what!? He was! He said he'd love to do it again sometime. In fact, he wanted to fix a date and time there and then. I quickly came down from cloud nine and found my voice again. Before I could think things through, I blurted

Marine Drive as it was back in the day

out presumptuously, "If I was to come out with you again, then I have a few conditions in mind. We can see each other on an on-going basis only if you have the same intentions as me." He seemed amused when I continued. "You see I'm of a marriageable age. I like you but I would agree to get to know you better if your intentions were to eventually settle down too. If you'd just like to date someone for the sake of it, then I would have to refuse right now. Let's go out for movies and to restaurants etc. and see if we're comfortable with each other, keeping that in mind. If we find that we're not suited to each other, we can then part as friends."

He gulped down his coffee to reply. "Of course, I have similar interests. I mean I would love things to work out between us for the long term. Please, tell me how much time you need to get to know me. Shall we say six months? Would that be enough time?" I smiled and nodded in agreement and so began my whirlwind courtship days with Rony.

Besides the regular cinemas and restaurants, he'd take me for long walks down Marine Drive. We'd walk down the flyover, one of the oldest ones in the city today, watch the birds fly over the horizon, the pigeons aflutter, and stroll along the promenade.

Our favourite pass time was to buy the boiled 'Channa' or the 'Sheng' from the old vendors, 'Sheng-Channawallahs' who'd come around faithfully with their big baskets, homemade charcoal heaters all in one, strapped around their necks, calling out their wares to hungry passers-by. We could never resist the temptation. There was nothing like the taste of good crisp groundnuts just out of the 'tava'. All the vendors recognised us, as we were their favoured regulars. Sometimes they would throw in a 'Sukha Bhel' for good measure. "Salaam Saab, aaj kya lenge aap?" (Salutations sir! What will you buy today?) Came their familiar and friendly greeting. Rony was always one to make friends.

He'd ask them where they were from, whether they were married or had a family and take an active interest in their lives. They could feel his genuine warmth and concern and you could make out that all of them had a special liking for him. He almost never took the change back from them and when I questioned him, he'd just say, "Forget it. That money means more to him than me." Rony had some magnanimous qualities. He and I were different in so many ways but we understood each other and connected on the same wavelength somehow. He was the most understanding person I had met. He'd see things from a broader perspective and never failed to put people and their feelings before material things or his own ego. He was larger than life. I slowly came to appreciate his generous ways, his broadmindedness and his genuine involvement with people in general. I learnt from him and we grew together.

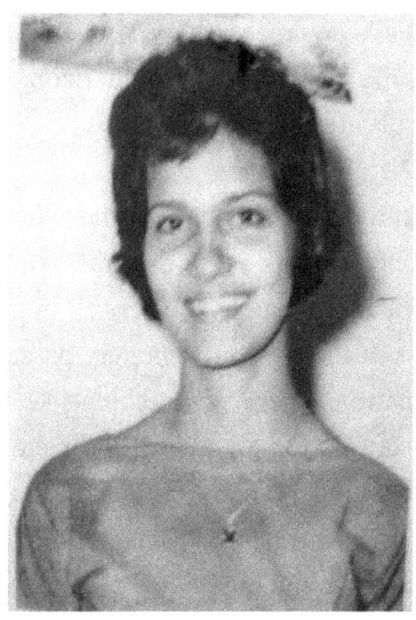

The photograph Rony requested and slipped into his pocket

I used to wait for him by my window. In those days, we didn't have phones at home so we'd rely on making dates and sticking to them. So, if he was late, I'd be all ready and waiting anxiously to see him turn around the bend in the distance. I'd run down so he wouldn't have to come up and waste time on niceties with my family. The time I got to spend with him was precious. I remember the 1st day he came over to meet my folks to make it official or to tell them about his good intentions. He was on his best behaviour and for once he was looking very tidy. He was never one to fuss over clothes and he'd usually wear the 1st thing in his cupboard. I could make out that he had taken a special effort to get dressed this time. I could imagine his ever-helpful sisters deciding what he was to wear and making sure they pushed him out of the house in time to make his 'Meet the parents' appointment. He didn't seem nervous although he told me later that he was.

He chatted candidly about everything under the sun and my parents seemed to take an instant liking to his endearing manner. He was warm and came across as genuine and he put them at ease. While my mum went into the kitchen to bring out the snacks, he flipped through a photo album that was lying on the side table. He came across a passport size black and white photograph of mine. He took a fancy to it and gestured to me, inquiring whether he could keep it. I nodded quickly and he slipped it into his shirt pocket with one clean movement. No one noticed or so we thought. It hadn't escaped the keen eyes of my over protective brother Eric. So when Rony was ready to leave, standing at the entrance and everyone was exchanging pleasantries, Eric suddenly confronted him about the snap in his shirt pocket. "What do you have in your shirt pocket? Do you mind if I take a look?" Without further delay and not waiting for a response, he reached his hand over to Rony's pocket, pulled out the photograph and began waving it in front

A bridesmaid for Eric and Josephine on their wedding day in 1967

of his face. I had become crimson by then with embarrassment.

I tried explaining but Eric wouldn't give me a chance. He said in a serious tone. "What's this huh?" Rony was simply flabbergasted. He assured Eric that he had requested me to keep the photograph and it was Eric's turn to turn red when he looked around for my reaction and he saw me nodding desperately. He at once began apologising profusely.

Rony just laughed it off and said. "Hey forget about it! Milly is a lucky girl to have a brother like you. I don't think I'd have had the guts to do the same thing if I were in your shoes." That incident was not forgotten for a long time to come. Eric became famous among Rony's friends and family and the incident was related many times over at all parties and get-togethers thereafter; of course with a tinge of 'Mirchi-Masala' or their spicy two bits added in for a laugh.

Eric met Josephine, the vivacious one, I had mentioned earlier, from my school. Luckily our parents approved. They began dating and were married in 1967. Eric looked so handsome in that black, glossy suit! Just a year later they were to give birth to their first son, and we were all so excited as the pregnancy had gone smoothly and the baby was doing so well. However, the infant didn't make it due to umbilical cord complications during childbirth. They were devastated. We all were. They named the child Joseph and till this day remember and pray for his soul on his birthday.

But God is loving and compassionate, a few months later Josephine was pregnant again with a daughter, who they Christened Illona in October that year. She was a beautiful baby and the first grandchild in the Pinto home. I was made the proud Godmother and I enjoyed spending time with the little baby when I got back from school. She was adorable! When she grew a little bigger, I'd tell her stories and she'd be glued to my face and expressions so much that it was an incentive to keep changing my face just to see it reflect on hers as she cutely mimicked the expressions she saw!

Josephine was such a natural mother; so caring and nurturing and also always organised and efficient. She is such a terrific sister-in-law. She had 'fitted right in' with us and her love, concern and giving nature won our hearts. She was my confidante for many things and I relied on her like the sister I never had!

God Mother to Illona, my brother's daughter.

It was tough being apart from Rony, so often in the beginning. Rony had to attend a training course in fire fighting at the Marine and Merchant Navy School in Powai. It was more than two to three hours away from where I lived, in the suburbs. He stayed there during the week and would make it back to town only on the weekends to spend as much time with me as he possibly could. He had it pretty rough commuting all the way and being split between spending time at home and with me. He longed for a longer break and his weekends were precious to him.

After completion of the course, he was called away on another assignment for one year. We had been dating each other for about close to seven months by then. It was a Saturday, an unusually breezy evening, when we were strolling hand in hand, something he had to actually ask for permission to do in public, that Rony did the unexpected.

Suddenly, out of the blue, he very coolly slipped the question in between our conversation. Just like that! As if it were the most casual thing in the world. "So what do you feel about me? What do you think?" He asked me. "You've known me for more than six months he reminded me. You must have made up your mind by now. So what's the verdict?" I was quite taken aback that he had put me on the spot like that and I didn't want to be the one admitting my feelings for him first. But I was ecstatic. We were both clear by then that we wanted to take things further. I had been thinking about bringing up the topic but didn't know how. I acted rather blasé about it, though. In fact, I gave him a rather tough time.

I told him I was disappointed with his matter of fact proposal and that I was a true romantic and wanted it to be done the right way, if I was to consider it. Even while I was ranting and raving about how I'd dreamed of the moment and how he had gone and shattered that dream, he was down on 'bended knee' right there on the promenade in front of thousands of people. He made the most endearing but funny face you could imagine with eyebrows raised and hand in the air, he asked me in the most storybook-like, conventional way, "Mildred, will you marry me and make me the happiest man on earth?" I hadn't learnt the value of just staying in the moment and enjoying it for what it was. "Please stop or I'll run away from here and disown you!" I said hastily, looking around to see how many people were looking. There were amused faces all right and I wished that I hadn't opened my big mouth.

He finally forced me to give him an answer, "Don't just leave me hanging!" I had to say, "Yes!" but only later when we were sitting on a bench and no one was staring at us anymore. What a playful, exciting moment I had managed to botch up with my unnecessary embarrassment! If it were today, I'd have played along and made him dance a little jig before I conceded.

Since Rony had to leave shortly, we decided to have a small engagement party at my place. It was December 8th 1968. We invited only the family members and some of Ron's closest friends. Josephine designed my dress and stitched it too. It was a pastel pink with a Basque and cap sleeves; very simple but very elegant. I loved it. I combed my short hair down with a side parting and the locks pulled over my ears accentuating my cheekbones. It was the typical 60's look. I was pleased with my appearance in the mirror. But there was no time to waste on vanity. I had to get ready to get booked.

We cooked up some tasty Goan treats like 'Mutton Xacuti', 'Prawn Pilaf', and 'Goan sausage fry' and for dessert; we served 'Bebinca' – a sweet dish sinfully rich, lots of eggs and sugar made in layers. I helped to clean up my little home and we put up new curtains to brighten up the place. The bed linen had to be changed and that bathroom had to be made spotless. I didn't want my to-be in-laws to get a bad impression.

So the evening finally arrived and everyone came over. All of us were in high spirits, laughing and joking. We had a Parish priest come over to bless the rings and our future. I remember Rony had brought along this fancy camera and it even had a tripod stand attachment. We took two reels of photographs and I was thrilled, posing with Rony and the family. The dinner was scrumptious.

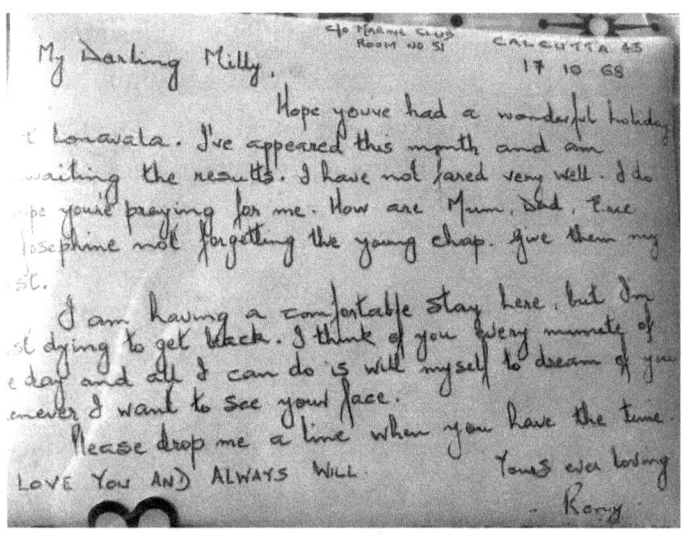

Treasured Postcards from a true romantic!

We had done it! We had committed our lives to each other and officially agreed to marry for better or for worse. So, the hunt for the perfect soul mate was over. We had found ours. I was 24 at the time and very much in love.

All the teachers were so surprised when they saw the engagement ring on my finger but they had guessed who the groom-to-be was. They had seen him come to school to pick me up sometimes. "So tell us all about him. What's he like? He's handsome. That we know!" I was never one to share much. So I guess I disappointed them with my "He's nice!" and that's that answers. "You must invite us to the wedding. So when is the big day?" they inquired holding my hand in theirs to get a closer look at the platinum ring studded with ten small diamonds. I was very proud of that ring especially as it looked like the diamonds went all the way around. I had ensured that the jewellery store set the diamonds so that it looked like it was an 'eternity' ring – quite the rage in those days. Life felt good. I felt happy with a certain kind of elation as if I was walking on cloud nine.

We had a very long engagement by normal standards. We didn't set a date immediately, as Rony wanted to complete his '1st officers' before we got married. But since everything happened so fast and we were dating for only about eight months before agreeing to spend the rest of our lives with each other, it turned out to be a time to get absolutely comfortable with the idea. In fact, Rony even had to go off abroad in between and our relationship became a long distance one. I'd wait for the postman to bring in letters from Rony that would now be addressed very endearingly, "My darling Milly", "Your loving Rony". I felt we belonged together and this made me very happy. I preserved all those descriptive love letters and cards. They became some of my favourite treasures.

It was a Thursday, mid March 1970. More than a year of being apart, when I got a telegram from Rony asking me to make arrangements for a visa for Hong Kong. Eric was well settled in Air India – the leading Indian international airline. He was given free airline tickets for his entire family as a perk of the job. So, we made arrangements to join Rony in Hong Kong for a week. This was to be my 1st trip to a foreign land and I was excited but even more because I was going to see my beloved again after so long. I quickly bought a few trendy trousers and blouses. I was keen to look my best.

The plane trip was all that I had imagined – Simply Exhilarating! The take off was scary and my heart was in my mouth but once we were settled in our seats and the airhostess came around with our refreshments, I felt more at home. Actually more like a queen on her way to be reunited with her king. I could imagine Ron's chubby adorable face. He had sent me some snaps. He had gained so much of weight. He even started sporting a full-grown beard. He was probably under the impression that it would make him look slimmer or hide the fat on his face. On the contrary, I felt it added a few years instead. He was only 27 at the time but the extra weight made him look 35.

I was hoping he'd have gone clean-shaven again. I preferred the sleek look to the gruff. Finally, the moment arrived. I waited with baited breath to get off the airline, onto the jetty and into the Hong Kong airport so that I could run into the arms of my fiancé who I knew would be waiting to pick us up. Eric was more pre-occupied with the airport, the beautiful shops, arcades, escalators, and expansive and utterly posh marble and granite floors. Pushing our trolleys was like sliding the wheels over ice. It was that smooth, clean and shiny.

Bell Bottoms and printed blouse. The glorious 70's in Hong Kong just before our wedding.

By now, I was scanning the entire visitor window near the arrival lounge to see if I could spot Rony's face. There was no sign of him. Eric was sure that he might have been delayed. So, we got out of the enclosure and started walking towards the taxi stands when all of a sudden a familiar voice shouted to us from behind. "I knew you wouldn't recognize me!!" "Hi Milly!" he said to me laughing aloud and running up to give me a big hug and a kiss. I was so overwhelmed. I could hardly believe my eyes. Rony was nothing like he was a year ago. He was so slim! He looked like a schoolboy!

We had completely missed him when we came out of the airport and had walked right past. He had wanted to see if we'd be able to recognize him. It was such a big and pleasant surprise! Apparently, he was determined to look smashing for his wedding as it was a once in a lifetime event. So he went on a diet and exercise regime using all the will power he had to lose the flab. For days, he'd stay on a liquid diet. I was worried about him crash dieting like that. It wasn't the best way to lose weight. But Rony assured me he was fine and we went on to have one of the best times of our lives. It was almost like a pre-honeymoon except Eric, my watchful brother was there to chaperone us.

We were to marry the week after we went back to Bombay. We shopped for the wedding. Rony was a spendthrift and he just loved lavishing us with all the treats of the city. We'd go to different eateries and sample authentic Chinese food. "Fly Lie" was the favourite. Time flies when you're having so much fun! We finally returned to India, to prepare for our wedding, held on the 18th of April 1970.

I can do all things through Christ, who strengthens me. Philippian's 4:13

Chapter 6

Hooked, Line And Sinker

There was so much to do: The dress, the accessories, the band, the reception hall, the decorations, the car, the invitations and the bridesmaids' dresses……. It was difficult cutting down on the wedding invitation list. Rony knew so many people and all of them felt very close to him. I had requested permission to use our St. Xavier's School hall for the wedding reception. It was their policy not to give out the hall for commercial purposes, but they made an exception in my case, which was a great boon as it was very difficult to get a reception hall at the last minute. You'd have to book much in advance.

I wore a simple long gown made of Hungarian silk. It had an elegant pattern with bell sleeves with a simple round neck. I wore a very classy jewellery set made of American diamonds set in gold; a necklace, a bracelet and earrings. I loved the way that set turned out. It was just what I wanted. I chose it myself from a design book. The matrimonial service took place in 'Our lady of Dolour's Church. We both belonged to the same parish. In fact, for a love marriage, we had everything perfectly matched as if it were a typical arrangement between parents. We belonged to the same religion, the same parish, and the same caste even! We were both Brahmins. Believe it or not, this caste system is so deeply rooted in our society even today and we even came from the same village in our native Goa; Sangolda in the Bardez district.

We were fortunate. It was a match that delighted both sides of the family equally. My parents couldn't have been happier. Initially though there was reluctance on my mother's part, as she knew what the life of a shippy's wife would be. Long periods apart and then there was also the danger of the rumours that went around about shippies in general. They were all known to have a woman in every port. I think it was a good lesson for me, to stop stereotyping or labelling people, based on other people's biased opinions. But once my parents knew Rony better, they were convinced that his love for me was genuine and felt reassured that he'd make a very good husband for their one and only daughter. On the topic of arranged marriages, it reminds me of what had transpired behind the scenes much before Rony and I had started dating.

Apparently, Rony had always had a soft corner for me right from the time he had spotted me when I was still in school, in the ninth grade. He had tried getting to know me better and even arranged for us to go out in a group but I always managed to foil his plans. In between, he had even started dating other girls but couldn't seem to get his mind off 'the impossible dream'. So, after he joined the Dufferin, he requested his parents to send a proposal to my place requesting my hand in marriage.

His parents were delighted with his choice and his father went all out to try and make his son's dream come true. They approached our family through a 'matchmaker' or a go-between, as they didn't know us very well. They had only seen us at church and we knew each other on an acquaintance basis alone. So when my mother was approached and was told the background of the 'boy' in question, she being aware of my constant reluctance to the arranged marriage scenario and her own belief that 'Shippies' were no good, took it upon herself to refuse the proposal without consulting me or even my father for that matter. "We don't want!" had prevailed yet again.

Rony's parents were very disappointed and felt bad to break the news to Rony who nonchalantly patted his dad on his back and said. "Don't worry about it, dad! There are many fish in the sea." But with that, he was even more determined to 'win me over' his way. There was to be no more Mr. Shy guy or conventional methods for him. He loved a good challenge but then again don't all men? That's when he began sending me greeting cards from exotic places with a return address at the back of the envelope hoping against hope that I'd reply and he'd get his green signal. But I was afraid to reply not wanting to let on that I liked him and mostly because I was intimidated by his writing skills. I was sure he'd be put off with my letters. I couldn't write to save my life and I felt it was better to appear impolite than foolish. But Rony was even more intrigued with my silence.

By then, the girl who he had been dating more frequently than others began to get very serious about him. He liked her company but he knew that she had second place in his heart and he couldn't live with that, knowing that his number one was still single and available. So, he decided that he should break it off with her before things became too serious and complicated. He hadn't even begun his pursuit of me and up till then had got only negative vibes from my side. But his faith and confidence of feeling held on and most of all he knew in his heart of hearts that it was the right thing to do. It wasn't one of the easiest no doubt.

The girl was naturally quite upset but appreciated his honesty and the fact that he didn't take advantage of her vulnerability. Knowing his side of the story was so interesting. It did wonders for my ego that's for sure.

So, the rest is history and there we were standing in front of the priest pronouncing our vows. "I take you, Rony to be my lawfully wedded husband, in sickness and in health, in good times and in bad, to love you, to cherish you and to honour you for the rest of my days till death do us part" I was nervous. I could hardly believe my own ears. I was actually saying those solemn words and jumping into the unknown. I prayed that this leap of faith would be the right one. I had spent many sleepless nights wondering what marriage would be like.

Whether or not I'd make a good wife, be able to look after another person other than myself, run a home, cook meals and clean, bring babies into the world. At times, I felt so scared and unprepared for one of the biggest decisions you make in your adult life. After all every other relationship in life, be it your parents, siblings are incidental or destined to be. The one choice, in my case that was truly my own, was the choice of a life partner and I had better be making the right one.

Rony was a special man in every way. He had a heart of gold. He was broadminded, intelligent and humorous; one of the most generous men I had ever come across. I knew I loved him but there were other things to consider like his fondness for the good life: drinking, smoking and socialising. In that sense, I was the complete opposite. I preferred quiet evenings with him alone and hated going to parties where all you ended up doing was making small talk or seeing grown men babble on about God knows what.

I wasn't very comfortable with a few of Rony's friends. I wasn't sure how genuine there were. I remembered that awful night on Christmas day when Rony had come down after a long stint of more than a year on board the ship. We were engaged at that time and I was so happy to go to the dance with him at the Catholic Gymkhana, a favourite club where youth and older generation alike hung out either to play billiards, badminton, snooker, tennis, basketball, cards or housie. My teacher friends were also going to be there and I was looking forward to showing off my fiancé. The exact opposite happened. Rony got high on alcohol and very carried away with his other drunken friends. His sister had also come along with us and we were both pretty embarrassed with their behaviour.

There was another girl in our group who had joined us with her date. Roger, a friend of Rony's, fancied her and requested her to dance. He was reeking of whisky and so she refused. Rony took it upon himself to make his friend feel better so he said in a loud voice. "Don't worry Roger, I'll dance with you."

They staggered across the dance floor hand in hand, singing aloud and making an absolute spectacle of themselves. I didn't know where to look. I wished that the whole ground would open up and swallow me up right there and then. Rony knew very well, even in his drunken stupor that I was upset; make that hopping mad. I scowled and sulked the whole evening and was even angrier when Rony didn't seem to care. Even when we were all making our way home, he walked right in front, leaving me behind to fend for myself with no one I was comfortable with.

I was so annoyed that tears had begun to sting my eyes. We walked down my street at 2.00 am in the morning in deathly silence, what seemed to be a never-ending walk. He didn't say a word and nor did I. When we reached the entrance to my building, he asked if he should come up and I just shook my head in response. He seemed annoyed that I was behaving like a stuck up. He mumbled something about me being a 'Puritan'. I didn't waste time going up and heard him say, "Goodnight!," in a curt tone.

I couldn't sleep that night. The whole night I just lay awake tossing and turning, crying and sobbing; my mind rushing through a million thoughts. I knew I wouldn't be able to live with a man who had so many vices. I had never seen this side of Rony but I had to be aware that this was also a big part of his life. I wouldn't be able to stand his smoking or drinking and who's to say whether our love would fly out of the window once we were married. Maybe he was even worse than what I had seen and perhaps that glimpse was just the tip of the iceberg. My mind felt like a whirlwind but by the end of it, I realised what I had to do. I loved Rony but love was not enough. I met him, as we had decided, the next day in the evening. My eyes were still swollen and my face was all puffy, which was a dead giveaway that I had been crying my eyes out!

Rony was very apologetic about the previous night and the perfect gentleman again. But before he could say much, I simply slipped the engagement ring off my finger and placed it on the table in front of him and said. "I can't marry you. It wouldn't work. I guess I am too prudish for you." I proceeded to explain further but Rony put up his hand in a gesture to stop me from saying anything more. "I love you." He said. "And there is nothing I want more than to make you my wife. I behaved like an idiot and I deserve this." He said pointing towards the ring. "Drinks did this. I promise that I won't touch another drink or smoke. He butted out the cigarette that was in his hand and he took the ring and slipped it back on my finger.

"All I'm asking for is another chance. You won't be disappointed. I give you my word." I could see the sincerity on his face and I believed him. I saw that I had got through to him. He knew that he could actually lose me and he respected my decision to break off the engagement. He realised how much of guts it must have taken for me to do what I did. I had stood my ground in spite of the possible scandal that would have been attached to my name or that I would also drag my family name down too. Breaking off an engagement was big news and our entire community would have been wagging their tongues, mulling over the causes of the split. Not to mention that I'd also have to deal with my broken heart and go through the torture of being without the man I was so much in love with.

Rony's respect grew. He fell deeper in love with me and was even more convinced that he'd do anything to make it work. I was relieved that he didn't accept the ring back. I gave in to my heart rather than my head. I melted like butter and I never felt happier to have resolved one of our first 'fights'. As he slipped the wedding band on my finger more than a year later, I felt so overwhelmed. I knew I had made the right choice and I believed we were meant to be together.

His eyes spoke of sincerity and his face glowed with happiness. "I do," I said and I meant every word of those vows. I do believe that my mother was right when she said, "If Rony is the man for you, he'll still be there at the right time." I was 25 years old and mentally ready to take on the responsibilities of true adulthood!

The Barbara Streisand song 'The Way We Were' comes to mind when I look back at those happy times…

Misty, water colour Memories.....

Of the way we were!

Scattered Pictures!...

Of the smiles we left behind...

Smiles we gave to one another...

For the Way We Were!

"If I have the gift of prophecy and can fathom all mysteries and all knowledge, and if I have a faith that can move mountains, but do not have love, I am nothing." – 1 Corinthians 13:2

"Entreat me not to leave you, or to turn back from following after you; For wherever you go, I will go; And wherever you lodge, I will lodge; Your people shall be my people, And your God, my God. Where you die, I will die, and there will I be buried. The Lord do so to me, and more also, If anything but death parts you and me." - Ruth 1:16-17

"In the same way, you husbands must give honour to your wives. Treat your wife with understanding as you live together. She may be weaker than you are, but she is your equal partner in God's gift of new life. Treat her as you should so your prayers will not be hindered." - 1 Peter 3:7

"Love is patient, love is kind. It does not envy, it does not boast, it is not proud. It is not rude, it is not self-seeking, it is not easily angered, it keeps no record of wrongs. Love does not delight in evil but rejoices with the truth. It always protects, always trusts, always hopes, always perseveres. Love never fails" - 1 Corinthians 13:4–8a

Chapter 7

Reality Bytes

Every girl has images in her mind's eye about what marriage will be like. In most cases, we tend to dream about Mr. Right. We visualize his physical looks and personality and imagine ourselves being swept off our feet. But in reality, no matter whether we've fallen in love or whether our parents fixed us up with their idea of an ideal husband, once the fairy tale wedding is over, we land squarely on our feet, firmly on the ground after that temporary walk on cloud nine. Few fairy tales tell of what happens after 'they lived happily ever after.' We grow up on these tales, watch romantic movies and love to feed ourselves with the mush. Very few of us are actually equipped to handle the many adjustments that marriage brings.

You've hardly got acquainted with your husband; his mannerisms, moods, hobbies, quirks, needs and desires when you discover you're pregnant with your 1st child and there's no time to be anything but overjoyed. Your body starts changing, rebelling, you're spewing your guts out in the mornings but everyone is simply bubbling over with happiness. So on one hand you're adjusting to the rapid bodily changes and on the other you're still in the process of getting used to your new family, your in-laws, the new kitchen laws and your man. If you're not a superwoman, then who is?

The 1st few years of marriage for me weren't all I thought they would be. Adjusting to a new home was hard enough but having to do it without your husband around is much tougher! Rony was not as financially stable as he'd have liked to be. We spent on the wedding and the honeymoon. We went to the south of India and toured Ooty,

Mysore and Bangalore. It was hot as it was in the middle of summer, but a lot of fun. The place is lovely, greenery stretching out for miles and picturesque landscapes all around.

We visited the sites, went for boat rides, elephant rides and took a whole series of photographs near all those exotic statues of ancient queens and kings. We had pre-booked a nice lodge and we met other honeymooning couples on the trip, which added a different flavour to the experience.

With the Pereira's - my new family

I enjoyed being with Rony and simply loved the time we spent away from it all. It was almost surreal. But that's what honeymoons are. It's like a whole different world and you just wish it would never end. Like all other good things, our honeymoon too came to an end and before the month end, Rony had to go abroad on an assignment for a couple of months. I felt lonely. I wished Rony was home. I was expecting our first baby and I needed his tender, loving care.

Rony's father, Albert was a gem of a man. He was warm and gentle and would wake up early in the morning to make me an egg flip. He'd come over to me and gently put his hand on my head softly whispering, "Bai!, Bai! Here have some of this." He affectionately called me "Bai" which meant little one. I warmed up to his affectionate ways almost instantaneously.

My sisters-in-law were both a few years younger than me, in college and ever ready to have some fun. They were like real sisters to me and we bonded very quickly sharing some of their best-kept secrets and girly stories. The youngest liked to pretend she was lecturing a huge class of aspiring hopefuls and I'd pose as one of them asking her questions to make it more authentic. She was a live wire and made sure that all of us were in splits of laughter when we were together. She'd organise movie outings for us three. It was such fun!

My in-laws were so welcoming and really nice yet I'd long to go back to my home. I'd leave early in the mornings to attend mass and then run over to my mother's place to have hot 'chapattis' with cream and sugar and my mum's tea. I'd make sure that I went back within the hour so nothing seemed out of the ordinary.

One evening in August when Rony was down after a long stint, we were all sitting around in the hall, cracking joke after joke. Rony as usual was relating all the stories about his escapades on-board and offshore. Rony's older brother was also keeping us in hysterics with his imitation of the old 'Padres' in Goa. "Hallao ek padre ani hallao ek deeonchar....ougdas ha?" He'd speak his broken Konkani as if he knew it at the back of his hand and we'd have tears in our eyes and a pain in our stomachs from laughing so much.

The only one who was not so amused was my mother-in-law. Mum wished that we'd not spend our time on mindless chatter. She announced that she was going out to attend a funeral service and would be back in an hour. She requested me to fry the 'chapattis'. The dough was already kneaded and ready. I agreed willingly. I was happy that she'd actually asked me if I could help out. She even double confirmed with me just before she left the house. "Are you sure you'll take care of it? Otherwise, I'll ask one of the girls to do it." She said. I knew that my sister-in-law had an exam the next day so that was the last thing she would want to do. I nodded affirmatively and she left.

So, we continued our chitter-chatter, but I had my eyes on the clock. I knew I needed about half an hour to complete all the 'chapattis' before she got back. So, when it was 7.30 pm I got up to go into the kitchen only to be yanked down by Rony's brother. "Where do you think you're going Milly?" he said. "Don't worry about those 'chapattis', we'll eat bread." All the rest joined in and agreed that they were not interested in the chapattis anyway and Rony too said I should forget it. They didn't want me to miss out on the interesting conversation. Rony even suggested that he'd help out later if need be.

So, I decided to stay for a little while longer and slip in a little later just before she came back so that I'd be in the process of making them at least. One hour came and went and we were still having a great time talking about the glorious past and how the Pereira boys had wrecked havoc during their Goa holidays trying out a gun given by their relative, Constantine, being chased by their grandma and how Rony was so chubby when he was young, he'd invariably get caught first and go about with red buttocks thereafter.

They were laughing about how they could write a book on 'A thousand ways to avoid punishment' when Rony's mother returned to find that the dough was as it was on the kitchen table. She was livid. She didn't say a word to me, but I knew by the look on her face. She called her daughter in a firm tone.

It would have been much easier to handle if she just yelled at me directly and got it over with. Instead, she preferred this cold war, which was unbearable. I had lost my appetite. When the rest offered to explain to her that they didn't want 'chapattis', she just ignored their explanations and went off without so much as an acknowledgement.

'Chapattis' 'Chapattis', I was beginning to dislike the very mention of the word. I was helpless and everyone just continued with his or her day as if nothing was amiss. To them, it was a triviality, but to me, it was an obsession. Why couldn't anyone see the battle? - Realise how upsetting it was? I felt alienated and terribly miserable.

That night I told Rony about the incident. He was tired and just thought I was making a big deal out of nothing. He advised me not to take things too seriously. But it was easier said than done. I kept taking everything personally and my mind played havoc. I have realised over time that most of our needless stress is created in our own minds. Being able to manage and control our own thoughts is half the battle won literally!

A few days later, we had just finished a very late lunch. Rony had over eaten as usual, as his mum would insist that he eat second and third helpings. He had gained all the weight he had lost at our wedding. He weighed more than 85 kilos and his face had become round and puffy. I tried intervening only to hear, "Let him eat. He doesn't get good home food on the ship." If she only knew that he was gorging himself with the best of foods while on board and that he took second helpings only to please her.

I knew that he was doing so at risk to his own health. In fact, he'd always say that if he didn't do something drastic to control his diet, drinking and smoking, which he had taken to again, he'd be a likely candidate for a heart attack. I was afraid that he was heading in that direction and I felt helpless.

Living with his parents didn't make it any easier as I didn't feel comfortable to express my opinion firmly. Teatime came and mum suggested that I go get the biscuits from the cabinet for Rony and dad. Since we had eaten such a late lunch, I knew that Rony wasn't interested in the biscuits but I asked them both all the same. They declined, saying that they were too full to eat another morsel.

Mum came back into the room and seeing that the biscuits were still not brought to the table, asked me why I hadn't got them yet. There was something about the disapproving look on her face or maybe it was just a build up of the many other similar occasions, which made my mind reel. Something snapped within.

Before I could stop and rationalize any further, I stomped into the kitchen, forcing the cabinet door open, grabbed the biscuit tin, slammed the door shut and banged the tin on the table top next to Rony and dad. "HERE ARE YOUR PRECIOUS BISCUITS," I shouted out loud with tears already welling up in my eyes. With that, I marched away in a huff to the bedroom and began packing to leave.

My emotions were playing havoc. I blame my expectant state & those raging hormones. I cringe to think how awful my behaviour was! When you're that young, you simply can't comprehend what it's like for a mother to hand over the caretaking to her daughter-in-law. You're not sure she would do as good a job as you would for your son. If I knew then, what I know now about what a long way a little warmth and a few appreciative gestures make, I am pretty sure the situation would have been a lot different. All I knew was how difficult the change was for *me,* but I'm sure it was for her too.

I made a mental note, if and when I became a mother-in-law one day, I would try my best not to interfere. I would be available when they needed me but would respect the phase of life they were in and let them live it. I also felt more certain that I would not expect, but instead, encourage my son to live separately when he got married. Things have changed with every generation and more couples nowadays prefer to live separately.

Rony tried convincing me out of it but he knew better to attempt to calm me down in the mood I was in. He had never seen me like this and he thought it better that I had a break in any case. I went to my mother's place. Rony was supportive throughout that phase. He even came over to our place and lived with us. Our place was so tiny and it was an inconvenience to not only my folks but mostly to him. He wasn't used to such small spaces or my father's rules. The bedding had to be put with the same face up every night and Rony could never be bothered to notice the difference but he made sure he did.

Another adjustment was my father's insistence on timings. Everyone had to awaken at a certain time, have a bath at a certain time, eat meals at a particular time and sleep at an appropriate time. I respected Rony's open-mindedness during that period, as I hadn't been half as cooperative in his home. It was an eye-opener.

I needed his support and understanding and that's exactly what he gave me. We spoke about the scene I had created at his place only much later when I brought it up and apologised for the way I had acted. I was sorry to have misbehaved like that, especially in front of dad, Rony's father. I loved and respected him a lot and he was the last person on earth that I intended to hurt.

We used to visit them now and then but I couldn't bring myself to apologise to his mother, my pride clouded my better judgement, which I regretted and he never forced me to. Rony was determined to start saving to buy a new home for us. But we were in no way ready to live separately as yet.

Rony had been overjoyed when he first heard the news of my pregnancy. He couldn't wait to be a father. He treated me like a queen. I felt really special but it's hard dealing with the changes; the hunger pangs, nausea and vomiting in the beginning, the mood swings, the sudden inexplicable depression, the weight gain and the swollen feet. On one hand, it was exhilarating to be bringing another human being into the world. But on the other, it was scary and I felt vulnerable and uneasy about how our lives were about to change completely.

Our parents were very happy to hear our big news and it sort of brought about a new bonding between the two families. Josephine helped me stitch some cute baby dresses and nappies for the baby in preparation for his or her arrival. I wondered if we would have a girl or a boy. Rony was more concerned that we have a healthy baby irrespective of the gender. He just wanted everything to go well with the pregnancy and the delivery. I was due mid-January of the following year.

I started reading books on pregnancy and so did Rony. He believed in reading everything he could get his hands on so that he was always well informed. He knew the stages of my pregnancy better than I did. He was able to understand my mood swings and even predict what I'd feel during each month. I got so used to being cared for and being able to be myself that it was awful when he had to go away to sea during the mid-semester of the pregnancy.

His father was so concerned about me. He'd go out of his way to see to my every need. I grew very close to him during those days. He was a soft, warm-hearted man. He had the most caring eyes. He was stately about six feet tall, lean with silver hair always combed neatly in a side parting. He had a handsome face and a defined jaw line and the distinctive 'Pereira' nose.

Rony's father, Albert was a banker by profession. He was well respected in his circles and looked up to by most. He provided well for his large family and gave of his time. He was meticulous, disciplined and orderly in his ways. He'd keep accounts of everything, pay every bill on time and budget perfectly each month. Rony was just the opposite. He'd be the happiest if someone took care of the mundane chores for him. He couldn't be bothered about what he wore or where his important papers were.

So I guess you could say he didn't take after his dad in that respect. His father was very patient with him, however. He'd ensure that Rony's shoes were polished, his papers were in order and his white shirt was ironed and kept ready on a hanger the previous day. He'd remind Rony of the things he needed to take care of and try and get him to make it on time. With Rony, it was always last minute.

I began taking over these responsibilities from his dad. Someone needed to 'look after him'. I listened when he wanted to talk, I warmed his food when he came back late at night, I'd wait up for him. I enjoyed accompanying him to cricket and football matches and even picked up phrases and after analysis on each sport including tennis and billiards.

Rony loved to play billiards at the Marine club or the Catholic Gymkhana. He'd become very good at the game and I'd watch with pride when he'd pocket ball after ball, his face tight with concentration. Rony also liked a good gamble. He'd place bets with his competitors. Win some and lose some was par for the course. We'd all get a special treat on the day's winnings at the end of the evening.

Money would never manage to stay in Rony's hands. He made sure he spent every penny. He lived extravagantly; always got into cabs, ate out most of the time, treated his friends a lot and bought expensive gifts for them and extended family, my family included.

The irony is that on the face of it, you would consider Rony to be a man of this world; A person who enjoyed the good life, but the paradox was that he never really seemed to care about money that much. Unlike the rest of us who valued it so much and felt the pinch each time it left our palms, he had no attachment to it. When it was there, he spent it. He made sure everyone around him was having a great time. Even when it wasn't there, he'd have the same attitude. He'd give the last shirt on his back if required. I wondered who was more materialistic: was it he or I?

He was always the first to apologise in our relationship. He was a big man with a big heart and I appreciated his maturity. I needed him to understand my moods and he was extremely insightful, caring and open-minded.

I felt happy because he was so ecstatic. His enthusiasm was always infectious. I felt surer of my own ability because of his constant reassurance. I was so glad when Rony arrived. I had missed him so much. He had come like a Santa Claus with lots of baby stuff. The excitement we both felt was welling up.

That whole season was great fun and with Rony around there was never a dull moment. His laughter and the many outings added to the fun. We enjoyed Christmas together. It was a cosy and very special period for us with the baby on the way. We thought of names for boys and for girls. He'd even sing to the baby; strum his guitar next to my stomach saying, "This one is for you." We could feel the baby respond. I'd gently place Rony's hand on the spot on my belly where the baby was kicking. The feeling was unmatched!

One afternoon on the 20th of January, while I was lying down in our bedroom, I noticed that the bed was damp and looked down to discover that my water bag had broken. I shouted out to Rony, "This is it. Let's go to the hospital. Call Dr. Winifred" Rony was in a spin. He had to consciously cool down and get us organised. He helped his sisters pack a few essentials with my directions and we all took off for Elizabeth nursing home, a privately run hospital near hanging gardens.

My gynaecologist was a very good doctor. I had immense trust in her professionalism and she made me feel very relaxed and comforted. I was admitted into a private room and immediately taken into the theatre for labour. There were long agonising hours of breathing and puffing but the joy of the finale is better than any other euphoria you've ever felt and the painful hours prior to it are quickly brushed aside. The small wonder with tightly clenched fists, eyes shut and all red with the first burst of air through his lungs was here. Yes! A perfectly healthy seven-pound baby boy; my very own little bundle of joy!

"Have you not read that he who created them from the beginning made them male and female, and said, 'Therefore a man shall leave his father and his mother and hold fast to his wife, and the two shall become one flesh'? So they are no longer two but one flesh. What therefore God has joined together, let not man separate." - Matthew 19:4-6

Chapter 8

Parenting – An art form!

They placed him next to me for a few minutes before taking him away to be washed and swaddled in fresh linen. I put my little finger into his palm and he held it tightly. I loved the feeling and I felt a soft warm feeling within that left me spellbound. He was so perfect in every way. He had small fingers with the tiniest nails and round face with a significant amount of hair on his head. I looked for the family trademarks like the large 'Pereira' nose and I even went so far as to pry his eyes open to see if he had inherited his father's light eyes. I so wanted him to have those unique crystal greys. No such luck! His eyes were jet black like mine. I must admit I was a wee bit disappointed.

Rony was transformed into a child himself. He looked down proudly at his son with his jaw clenched as if he was biting his own tongue to keep from squeezing the little fellow's tender hands. He came out with the most unheard of endearments coined exclusively for his 'babush', 'shamshababbums' and 'lil shanna boy'. We stayed at the nursing home for a few more days before we brought the baby home for the first time. My sisters-in-law had arranged the room for us with all the baby's things and the crib next to our bed. Mum and dad were delighted and went out of their way to see that everything was taken care of. We got an 'aaya' to come home every day to give both the baby and me an oil massage. She'd help me give the baby a bath too.

A week later, we decided to Christian our new-born son and on Rony's request, we named him Albert Valentine Do Rosario Pereira. Albert was Rony's father's name and since he happened to be born on my dad's birthday, we chose his first name as our son's second name Valentine. The Do Rosario came down from the family ancestral lineage. It also happened to be my mother's father's birthday too. So, it was a special day and it seemed as if all his ancestors were giving him their blessings in a special way. We dressed Albert in a long Christening dress made from my wedding dress.

We requested Rony's younger sister to be his Godmother and my brother Eric to be his Godfather. They were witnesses at the ceremony at our Lady of Dolour's Church. We decided to have the Christening party immediately as Rony was leaving to join the ship. He was overjoyed and couldn't wait to celebrate!

Mum's place with Albert aged 6 months.

Meanwhile, I wasn't feeling too well myself. I was constipated and had a severe headache. I had told the nurse before leaving the hospital. She gave me a few Dulcolax tablets to relieve the pain. I took them all in one shot mistaking them to be a prescription. In a couple of hours, Albert began to dirty his nappies one after the other. He was crying nonstop and we couldn't wash and dry his nappies in time. We had to finally tear up a bed sheet to make makeshift nappies for him. We were wondering what set the loose motions off and called the doctor. He asked me what I had eaten that day. Suddenly I remembered the tablets I had taken and he said that since I was nursing Albert, the tablets were the cause. He asked me to give him as much water as he could possibly retain or else he would go in for dehydration. I was really worried.

Some Christening party it turned out to be. It was a nightmare. We gave him the medicine the doctor prescribed and I stopped breastfeeding him.

We fed him lots of water. He didn't sleep the whole night and all of us were exhausted. The next day he seemed to get better. He slept for four hours at a stretch. Such a helpless little one! My heart really went out to him.

I missed Rony greatly when he was away and I knew that Albert did too. I'd often get into the self-pity mode. I'd find myself crying about every little thing. I had become even more sensitive after the delivery.

I longed for Rony to be there so I could talk to someone and let off steam. I'd speak to Josephine whenever I got the chance. She and I had become close. She was always involved, concerned and went the extra mile, in spite of her busy schedule, to help out in any way she could. She was a very giving person and I admired her spirit in many ways.

One day in April, I got a telegram from Rony informing us that he was to bring in the ship to the port of Goa and that he felt I needed a break. I had written to him all about the sleepless nights, the colic, the diarrhoea and how I wished he were there to shoulder some of the responsibility and how I felt sorry for myself. He insisted that I bring Albert along and come to Goa to spend time with him while they were docked at the port.

He said he would be able to manage some time off to go ashore while the cargo loaded. I was afraid we wouldn't be able to manage with Albert being just three months old. He was not in the best of health to travel and how would I manage the feeds, the sterilisation, the medicines, warming the milk etc. But Rony would not hear anything further.

I was on my way to Goa. It was absolutely fantastic meeting Rony after so many months. We had missed each other and he'd been longing to spend time with Albert, watch his progress, play with him, sing him bedtime lullabies and rock him to bed. He so wanted to be part of our lives at every stage. I assured him that child care was much more than all those good parts he missed and boy did he get a taste of the 'package deal' I warned him about.

We stayed at a hotel, close to Rony's ship in Margao, south of Goa. It was summer and actually the worst time to be in Goa. The sun was intense and the heat was unbearable. Close to 40 degrees Celsius and dry. We'd keep the coolers on in the room the whole day and we were given a car by the company, so on weekends, Rony would drive us around sightseeing. Having a three-month-old with us didn't deter Rony from going ahead with plans and he didn't shy away from stopping at strangers' houses. In a way it taught me how to just go with the flow and find a way to do what we had to, to enjoy ourselves, something I would never have considered if it was not for him.

I had stopped breast-feeding Albert after the near dehydration he went through when he was hardly a week old. The doctor advised that my milk would be too strong for him to resume after being off it for a while and that he ran the risk of a relapse. In fact, after a few months, I stopped lactating.

I thought that just being with Rony would make everything better. But my mood swings didn't go away. It almost seemed like I was taking this opportunity to pour out all my pent-up frustration to Rony. Albert would cry the whole night, wake up at short intervals and I could not get one night of peaceful sleep. Very often Ron would beg me to take it easy assuring me that he would take care of Albert, but I was a light sleeper and I knew he required my attention.

Besides Rony was a novice at handling Albert's crying fits. I'd diligently awaken, warm his milk, cool it and put him on my lap to rock him to sleep again. The minute I'd attempt to put him down again to sleep, so I could at least stretch my legs, he'd begin bawling out again. Rony watched this for a while and gave me quite a telling off. "Put him down and let him cry". He said in a firm voice. "No wonder you've been spending sleepless nights. You've thoroughly spoilt him. He's playing up because he's used to your constant mollycoddling. Let him get used to being by himself for a while." With that, he took Albert from my lap and placed him down next to us and patted him with a firm hand.

I looked at Rony and thought "What a heartless man I've married. He doesn't even care about his own flesh and blood. My poor little baby." But it wasn't even a few minutes before Albert stopped weeping from pure exhaustion, he began to whimper very softly and soon fell asleep. I was amazed. Rony had achieved the impossible according to me. All these torturous months, I had rocked him night after night on my lap and I was exhausted. We slept better that night and after having tried the same thing for a few nights, Albert learnt that no amount of his crying and yelling was going to make his mother concede, he slowly gave up his tantrums and would sleep all by himself eventually.

Rony did a whole lot of reading on parenting; baby care, post-natal care and he always seemed to know more than me on almost every subject. Sometimes he'd be everything to me – my husband, my friend, my confidante and my father–figure all rolled into one. I found it very hard to imagine how I had actually managed without him all those months. He was my greatest help and I really did get time to relax and recoup with him around. He'd assist with washing the dirty nappies in batches and help me boil the milk and make Albert's feed, remind me about the medicine and take us out on the town too. I felt like an ingrate when I'd get into one of my moods and start crying for no apparent reason. He'd try to get me to speak about what it was I was feeling but I couldn't pinpoint why I was so depressed.

He even tried explaining that it was the hormones that were playing havoc and that it was mind over matter and that I had to at least try to control my mind from getting dragged into the negativity. His knowledge on my bodily changes made things easier for the both of us to handle those difficult situations. I didn't know why I was feeling so low. They now have a term for the condition I apparently had, 'postpartum depression'. I can never forget the afternoon, on one such unpleasant occasion, when Rony was tired with the stress both on the work front and personal one and he had not paid as much attention to Albert and me as I had wanted him to and I had gone into a bad mood as usual.

This time Rony was firm with me and told me to tell him what was bothering me or I could sit there and cry about it and he would never be able to help me. We were sitting together on the bed in the hotel room with Albert in between and my eyes and nose were red and my face was swollen; my trademark of a bad day. Sometimes I'd be embarrassed and think that others would probably go as far as to think that my husband was a rotten scoundrel and that he didn't take good care of his wife, which was so far from the truth.

I remember feeling neglected and sobbing from feeling sorry for myself when suddenly I felt a soft hand resting on my hand. I looked down to see that Albert had turned on his side and had rested his hand on mine and was looking up at me directly into my eyes with what I thought was the most adorable pleading look of compassion. It was almost like he was saying, "Don't cry, mummy. I'm here for you. You have nothing to feel sorry about."

My eyes shot up at Rony to see if he had noticed or seen what I had seen. "Did you see that?" He asked in wonderment. "Your son senses that you're feeling low. Why! He's actually comforting you! He's an intelligent and sensitive guy just like his father." He laughed and I had to share his joke. That little gesture did wonders for my mood. It took my mind off myself and I began to enjoy those precious moments with my beloved son and his humorous father. After all, days were numbered and I had to make the best of the few weeks I had to spend with Rony, where I had him all to myself. I had a lot of things to be grateful for as a matter of fact. The rest of that trip was a lot lighter and more fun. We spent more than a month together and Albert grew closer to his father. I was glad that a bond was being formed.

Albert was such a joy. Having a baby in the house is a fulltime entertainment but a lot of hard work too. One morning, a little more than a year later, I checked the calendar and realised that the due date for my monthly menstrual cycle had passed by four days. It was normally like clockwork and I could estimate the exact day I'd get it again the following month.

That morning, I felt my heart skip a beat or two. It was the all too familiar feeling of emptiness in the pit of your stomach and a need to gasp for air. "Oh No! It can't be". I thought, wanting to drop to the floor from sheer weakness in the knees. "I hope I'm not pregnant again. God please let it not be another pregnancy. Please!"

Albert was barely fourteen months old and had only just started sleeping eight hours in the nights without getting up at three and four in the morning. I had finally settled into a comfortable routine with him and I had begun enjoying myself again. I thought of sleepless nights, two babies to attend to, double the amount of dirty nappies, feeds in the middle of the night and I couldn't help feeling miserable.

Later, I double checked with the doctor and concluded that there was no escaping it. Nine more months of getting so heavy your feet swell and back to the maternity dresses. My mind started racing. I had to tell Rony. What was he going to say? Would he be surprised? Did I give away those maternity clothes and that crib? I'd have to get it out of the attic. Why me? I was so not mentally ready for a second child. Oh! How I needed a longer break.

I sent a telegram to Rony that evening. He was away on a trip, en route from Hong Kong to Manila. The message read, "We're going to have our second baby!" That night, the neighbours called me downstairs, as there was a phone call from abroad. I knew it was Rony and I ran to pick up the receiver. "Hi! Ron." I said. "It's true! I'm going to have our second. I'm pregnant!" I tried to whisper, not wanting the news to break in the building just yet. "I'm not thrilled and I was least suspecting it. I'll have to get mentally geared up I guess."

Rony was ecstatic as usual and I could only think "That's because you're not the one having the baby!" He was always one to think of the best. He seemed jubilant and he said, "The more the merrier! Let's have twelve at least! I love children. How are you keeping? Are you well? I'll try and get off early and be there for you this time." He said. "Take it easy! Eat lots of veggies and start exercising. Go for walks. It's good to be agile. It helps during the labour."

He babbled on and on and I have to admit his enthusiasm was infectious as always. I was glad the news had made him so happy. I felt guilty for having such a negative reaction. In a few days, I had settled down mentally and began feeling better about it. A lot of people said it was best to have the children one after the other so that they both go through common phases together and it was over and done with, at one shot. They'd grow up together and be companions to one another and how it was so important for a child to have a sibling more or less his own age. You tend to be less apprehensive the second time around. The experience and the dos and don'ts were so fresh in my memory.

Josephine was expecting her second too. On the 1st of October that year, she gave birth to a strapping little boy whom they named Ryan. He was a cute little chap with a round face and very cute, bright jet black eyes. Almost three months later, I felt a stirring in my stomach and thought it was best that I called Eric and Jo to take me to the hospital, as Rony was not in town. He was not going to be able to make it down for my second delivery.

It was the 23rd of December and I can never forget how beautiful the hospital looked that night as we entered Elizabeth nursing home, the same hospital where I had delivered Albert. The entrance was lit up with streamers and there were lights in the trees and on the sides of the building. There was a huge manger built in one corner of the reception area and an equally large, well-decorated fern Christmas tree. They had gone over board with creating the festive atmosphere and I felt so welcome.

My baby was going to be a special Christmas gift from heaven. I thought that if I could hold on for a day, she would be born on the Lord's birthday, Christmas day itself and how fabulous that would be. But the contractions started that same night and I went in for labour soon after I was admitted. The baby was born at 0250hrs on the 24th morning of Christmas Eve.

Noella's Christening. Holding her are her God Parents, Rony's Brother and youngest Sister

She was a beautiful cherub like baby girl with thick black-brown curly hair and big expressive eyes that were wide open from her very first moments in the world. She had a round chubby face and weighed 6 pounds and 2 ounces. When the Doctor brought her in after being weighed and washed, she said, "Congratulations Milly, you have yourself a little Noelle."

It meant Christmas child in French and later when deciding what to name the baby, I remembered the name that had sounded like it had a nice ring to it. I sent a telegram to Rony informing him that he was the father of a healthy baby girl and asked him which name he preferred Natasha or Noella – the two final short listed names we had all agreed upon. Six days had passed and there was no response from Rony. The following day, she was to be christened.

We all took a consensus and I decided to name her Noella. I liked the sound of the name and it seemed more appropriate since she was born on the eve of Christmas. The christening was special. I had made a very pretty long white dress for the baby and she looked like an angel. She was just that in fact. From the time she was born, she was no trouble at all. She slept peacefully for six hours and would awaken only at six for her feed. She'd only start whimpering a bit to remind me that it was either time for her feed, to be changed, or to be given water etc.

Compared to Albert and the time I had had with him, it was almost like she had come out with a super independent streak and an indifference of sorts, saying, "I'll show you! I won't be a bother at all!" She was such a pleasure looking after and I couldn't imagine how I had felt that I didn't want to have another baby. The joy out shadows the pain any day. I informed her Godparents to be on time. We had chosen Rony's youngest sister and his elder brother to be her God Parents and they were very happy to stand witness to what was a very enjoyable ceremony. "I hereby baptize you Noella in the name of the father and of the son and of the Holy Spirit, Amen." The priest proclaimed as he sprinkled holy water over her head. All she did was stir a little and move her face to the other side and continue sleeping. We all laughed and thought what a pity it was that Rony wasn't there too. When we reached back home, I saw a telegram from Rony on the table. I tore it open to read, "Name the baby Natasha."

One day, I got a telegram from Rony asking me to join him on board as they were to dock at Colombo, Sri-Lanka for a few days and sail for Singapore thereafter. I would need to get everything organised super fast so that I didn't miss the boat, literally! I was in such an awful predicament as Noella had caught a viral and was running a very high temperature. She had been ill for more than three whole days and my parents and I were worried sick about her. I had been staying over at their place for over a month.

I had no heart to tell Rony that I couldn't make it and besides, not only was I was yearning to be with him myself but was waiting to show off Noella to her father for the 1st time. He had not even got to see his little daughter since she was born. Much against my better judgement and to my parents' astonishment and anxiety, I decided to do the unthinkable. I packed every possible baby article I could

Studio Photograph sent to Rony of Noella's Christening.

think of, informed Rony's parents and set off on the trip to be with my husband, feverish baby and all. My parents called me selfish, heartless and irresponsible. "How can you take the baby when she's so sick? She'll probably get worse and you won't be able to forgive yourself if anything happens to her on the way." My father advised. But I had made up my mind and tried to rationalize that perhaps the clean air abroad would do her wonders. I hoped for a full recovery and I took all her medicines with me.

I wrapped her in warm clothes and took every precaution imaginable to ensure that she didn't become worse. We finally left and it was chilly on the flight to Madras but Noella slept well and the fever seemed to have dropped just above normal. I had to wait for four hours for the flight to Sri-Lanka, which only took off from Madras. It went well and Noella's fever was under control. When we reached Colombo, in fact, miraculously she seemed to be in good health.

What I had hoped for happened and I knew that God was with us throughout that journey. Rony was there to pick us up at the airport and he was looking so different with a full-grown beard and moustache. I almost didn't recognize him.

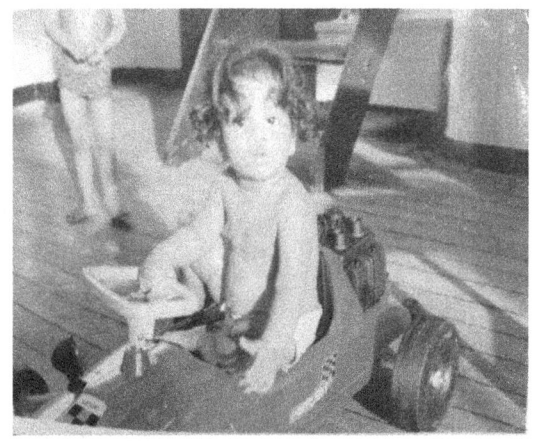

Noella taking a ride in her brother's favourite battery operated car on the deck of Rony's ship

He had eyes only for his daughter this time. He couldn't believe he had been part of such a perfect creation. It was almost difficult for him to imagine that he had created a person of another gender. He held her in his arms for the 1st time and his face was soft and tender smiling down at his angel. "She's beautiful," he said proudly.

Even as he made a fuss over Noella, Rony made it a point to catch hold of Albert and throw him up in the air, saying, "How's my Shanna boy doing huh? He's become a big boy and a big brother too no?" We both made a special effort to draw Albert into the limelight too so that he didn't feel that his new-born sister had stolen his parents' affection away from him. I kept explaining to him his role as a big brother and how he was now responsible to look after her, love her and take care of her by keeping a watchful eye on her at all times. He assumed the responsibility very well.

He was like my little helper. But looking at the two of them together made me happier than ever. I knew that God's timing was good and although we had not planned our second so soon, the age gap between the two and the bonding that was developing before our eyes somehow seemed perfect. "Mummy loves both of you very much."

On Rony's ship 'Hanciet'

I'd say and hug them together.

We spent many months on the ship sailing from one port to another enjoying a truly nomadic adventure. Rony would make it a point to select companies that allowed family to join him and he couldn't have been happier to have us around. He'd work diligently and spend an equal amount of time with us. Those were happy times and we were young parents, a couple growing more in love with each other as the days went by.

Everything was so easy on the ship. The provisions were taken care of. The cooks cooked us some delicious meals. We only had to make sure we went down to the pantry or mess as they called it, in time. The fridge was always stocked with the best stuff.

We used to have an Indian Chief Engineer on board and sometimes he'd bring his wife along too. It was nice having someone on board to talk to occasionally. Rony's ships were cargo carriers and we'd have to anchor or dock at certain ports of export and import for one month almost. We'd make trips ashore and do sightseeing or simply go on a shopping spree. Ron would buy the kids the best of toys and food and we'd take them to the malls and entertainment parks. We got thoroughly spoilt and enjoyed every minute of it.

Rony loved taking as many photographs as he could. We'd end up buying four rolls per trip and it was fun seeing the sights and reliving each moment captured forever. I used to forget there was any other existence besides our lives on board. I'd write back whenever I got the opportunity, to tell them how superb life was and to send them some postcards and snaps of the kids having fun.

Rony loved having them around. He'd play with them and allow them on the bridge and answer every inquisitive question about the instruments or the equipment on the deck or about the maps, sometimes over and over again. He'd take them piggy back, horsy-horsy and plane-plane, play football with Albert, small as he was or tell them bedtime stories. His stories were the best. The kids wouldn't let him sleep without one. He'd let his imagination run wild and get the kids engrossed in no time. They preferred his funny sounding names and unbelievable tales to the stories in the many picture books we bought them. They'd jump on his stomach and he'd bounce them up and down. He loved bathtub time.

They were all like little babies, including Rony, rollicking away in the water with lots of bubble bath froth and floating toys. They'd splash each other and sing songs for hours till their skin wrinkled from being in the water so long. Rony bought a battery operated red car big

Noella on her 1st Birthday on board

enough for Albert to get in and drive all over the bridge or deck.

Whenever we went ashore in Singapore, we'd get squeals of delight from all the young girls at the shopping centres or the restaurants. They'd all cluster around her and admire her curls and chubby cheeks. "She's a doll! She so cue Lah!" they'd exclaim in excitement.

We celebrated her first birthday cum Christmas on the ship. I dressed Noella in a fluffy white dress with red dots all over it and combed her curls in a fountain on the top of her head. I put on red shoes and a ribbon to match.

Life at sea was fantastic for the most part but not without the risk of course. I recall the close shave we had once which gives me the shudders just to think what might have happened to all of us. We were all sound asleep when suddenly there was a call from the bridge. Rony was startled and ran up to find out what the matter was. It was the dead of night around 2:00 am or so. In the near distance, the officer-in-charge had caught sight of an approaching vessel on the radar scanner. It was in close proximity and seemed to be approaching our ship headlong. We were cruising at around 22 knots at that point and the officer said he'd been trying without luck to contact the crew on board the other vessel.

Rony gauged the approximate speed at which the ship was approaching us and knew that there was every possibility of a collision if we didn't alter our course and speed quickly. He was worried but had to stay focused and think on his feet. They continued to contact the ship to no avail. After some 80 odd years of development, marine distress alerting still relied on a human being sitting in front of a receiver. The ship's

Radio Officers sent a distress message using Morse Code in the hope that the ship would hear the call and respond – Nothing!

Rony had to take proactive decisions. He ordered that our own ship change course and alter speed immediately. Given that we had very little time, he hoped that his plan would work. They altered direction to match the approaching ship but a vessel of that size and weight took time to change its direction. Rony sounded the emergency alarm and had everyone ready to jump ship with life jackets on, just in case. We watched with baited breath as the vessel came towards us like a shadowy death ship literally out of the blue; headlong at tremendous speed.

Our own ship grudgingly responded to the altered course that was set and what we all witnessed that day was nothing short of a disaster averted by the skin of our teeth. I kept praying, "Jesus protect us!" but everyone on board was white with fear.

We held our breath and finally applauded with relief as the ship passed us, now moving in the same direction, parallel to each other, so close, we could have jumped into it! Praise God! The collision was prevented. *His* protective mantle was around us that near fatal day. Thank God Rony had remained calm and was directed to take the right calls at the right time!

We've been through stormy nights where the rocking ship would leave us seasick yet the children found an opportunity to run from one side of the room to the other as if it were a joyride. Things would roll off tables when the ship tilted from side to side and they'd simply chase after it laughing merrily, oblivious of the looming danger, so blissfully unaware! In hindsight, life is very much like a voyage on a ship isn't it? I read somewhere a very appropriate quote, "A ship is safest in the harbour but it wasn't built for that." Our lives are like unique adventures with ups and downs, stormy at times and smooth sailing at others. But if we retain our awe, our wonderment and our child-like perspective, we could actually ride the stormy waves like a surfer seeking his next adrenalin rush; pushing ourselves out of our comfort zones is part of our growth.

Did I mention Noella was often in her own blissful world? Well one day, when we had gone ashore to stay in Singapore, she wandered off. I had taken the children to People's Park shopping mall and we were browsing when suddenly she went missing; just like that in a second! I was frantic! I searched for her everywhere and I couldn't find her. I began to imagine the worst as usual. What if someone had kidnapped her? Would I ever see my baby again! How was I going to tell her daddy that I had lost our child? Poor little Albert was exhausted as I kept running with him here and there, up and down the escalators to look for her on each and every floor.

Finally I approached the customer service and asked them to make an announcement describing her. Tears welled up in my eyes when I suddenly saw her little shoe lying next to a coloured stool in the store next to the one I had been browsing. I ran to it and found Noella sleeping peacefully behind the stack of stools. I picked her up and hugged her close out of pure exhilaration.

She gave us another scare, this other time on the ship. The children had been playing together – hide and seek and she hid away in the cupboard and refused to come out. Albert forgot about the game eventually. An hour or two later, when we couldn't find her anywhere, we began to get worried. I searched everywhere and called out to her but there was no response. Rony requested the crew to begin a search across the ship. Finally, after three hours of my hysterical pleas to turn the ship around to search the high seas for my baby, she emerged, nonchalantly and stood among the search party gathered in the cabin. Albert spotted her and cried, "Here she is, Mummy!" She claimed she was hiding but I suspect she might have had a nice peaceful sleep while all of us were out of our minds with worry.

Rony managed to complete his Masters despite having us around with him while he studied for it. It was like observing two sides to his personality. I'd watch him at his work, a mass of concentration while on the other hand he was like a little child when relaxing with us. To me, though, he was more of a man in every way. He never mixed the two. He was mature enough to leave his work stress at his desk and not have it filter into his personal life. His priority was always his family and we all felt his love and concern.

Albert and Noella in their favourite Super Hero T-Shirts.

The next five years we spent in and out of India. We visited Australia and saw the sights in Melbourne; we spent over six months in the U.K when Rony was on assignment on a ship that did not allow the entire family. Rony had hired an apartment in London where we set up a stopgap home. It was fun being on land for a change. I could take the kids to the park and to visit their cousins in Windsor. Rony's brother and his wife had settled there for good.

We had some memorable times in the UK. The children got to know their cousins better and they enjoyed playing together.

The same year, during the May holidays, we invited my mum to come down to the U.K to spend some time with us. She had not spent a lot of time with her grandchildren and I was keen that they grew close to her. The kids were very excited when I told them that she was coming down and even more ecstatic when they heard that Eric's son Ryan would also be accompanying her on the trip. They could hardly wait to see him.

Rony's brother organised some great trips for us. We went to Lourdes in France and visited Our Lady's grotto and bathed ourselves in the holy water. We went for a sightseeing trip around London too.

We stayed in England for just around two to three months, before we headed back to India for a holiday. Rony joined us and we stayed at the YMCA in South Bombay. Rony spent his evenings at the club playing snooker and billiards with the other shippies.

Rony was actually freelancing with various companies at the time and would go out to sea on short three-month stints; the way he liked it. He was becoming increasingly unsettled about leaving home so many times and hated being away from us. He spoke to me about his ideas of starting up something on his own. He wanted to get a little more settled and to spend some quality time with the children and to let them really get to know him and to be a good father. He thought that he'd sail for about a year or so and once he had saved a little money, he'd get himself a 'shore job' and have more time at home. He was offered a good assignment in Singapore to bring back a ship to Hong Kong.

The next project Rony took up was on board a relatively smaller cargo ship called 'Hanciet'. We sailed to Australia. On the second round trip, as soon as we arrived in Hodeida, the ship was surrounded; policemen came on board with an arrest warrant. Apparently, we learned that the company operating the ship had not paid up backdated arrears to the port so we ended up grounded in Hodeida for over three whole months.

One morning, while waking up to a leisurely breakfast, I was sitting by the cabin window, sipping my coffee, and staring out into the sky and the blue sea. It always had a calming effect on the nerves. My mind was at peace and I was meditative. Suddenly, in what seemed to be a long pause of time itself, where everything just seemed to come to a standstill, I saw an elongated full-length image of my father, a glow emanating all around his body, with a peaceful smile on his face, across the whole length of the sky. It was a gigantic, larger than life apparition almost.

He was looking directly at me. For the first time, I had actually got to see him smiling, no frown nor wrinkle on his forehead, without any care in the world. Throughout my life I had known him to be the worrier – Always bothered about something or the other, never took the time to just relax and enjoy the moment. It was a relief to see this image. I had often tried to make him see that there was no need for him to worry so much all the time.

As I wondered why that image had manifested along the skyline, my thoughts were interrupted by the buzz of the intercom phone. Rony answered it. It was the Chief Officer requesting him to come up to the bridge at once as there was an urgent telegram coming in for him from Bombay, India. Rony darted up and I wondered what it was about, it sounded serious. I didn't have a good feeling about it. In ten minutes, Rony returned with one of the most sullen faces I had ever seen. It was bad news. I was sure of that.

He didn't even look me in the eye; almost as if he wanted to avoid having to answer my inevitable questions. I was scared to ask what the matter was. I held his arm as he walked into the bedroom away from the kids who were oblivious.

We closed the door behind us. "What happened?" I asked softly. "It's dad," He said, his voice breaking. "He expired this morning." I squeezed his hand and said as a statement of fact, "My father." As the image flashed in my mind again. "No!" Rony said breaking down. "My father, not yours." There were tears in his eyes and I couldn't believe it. "Your dad? But….there's something wrong. I think it's my father. I saw…." I broke off seeing his pain. He gave me a look as if to say that my childish attempt at comforting him was quite uncalled for. I held him close as he sobbed softly, his head buried against my stomach.

My mind was in a tizzy. I had felt so sure it was my dad and not his. The image and the news seemed to match. I was feeling a deep sorrow within. "I have to send a telegram back saying that I won't be able to come down for the funeral. My God! I can imagine mum's state and I can't even be there." I kept silent. Somehow, I felt no words of comfort could do anything to ease the pain. The phone buzzed again. "One more telegram is coming through!" Rony seemed surprised and worried. He darted off to the bridge and I just sat there with a sinking feeling I could not understand. He came back a few minutes later. His face looked relieved but his expression was of concern and hesitation. "It's my father isn't it?" I said facing him. He just came forward and held me close against his chest. "I knew it all the time." I didn't cry. I just related the story to him. It was one of the strongest intuitions I had ever had.

He looked at me in amazement. "You're stronger than I am. Do you want me to send a telegram back? What do you want to say to mum, Eric and the family?" "I want to know the details. I knew he was not keeping too well. Was it a heart attack? He had high blood pressure which he was controlling with tablets and a restricted diet." I know he died peacefully. That image gave me the comfort I needed. I was brave in front of Rony. I knew the emotional rigmarole he went through thinking it was his father, then realising it was mine along with a sense of relief he also had to express sorrow. It was a difficult situation to handle for him and me but somehow I was given a special grace from God – one of the biggest fears of mine was the death of my loved ones – I was remarkably calm and this could only have come from the divine, in hindsight.

But that evening, I felt like being alone. I retreated to the cabin bedroom and wept as I thought of all the concern, warmth and affectionate moments I had spent with my father. Somehow, all his scolding, his strict exterior faded in comparison to the lighter moments. I mourned the loss of a father and a good man. We couldn't leave immediately so I could not be there for the funeral. Eric and Jo took care of Mum and all the arrangements. They were a source of strength to my mother.

We got a letter a fortnight later from Josephine regarding his passing and she told me how dad kept repeating, over and over again, "Praise you, Jesus! Thank you, Jesus!" Eric and Jo kept reminding him to pray and surrender so he did and it brought him solace. I was relieved to learn that he had died peacefully.

Soon we managed to get our release papers and the captain and crew were allowed to go back home. The agents even saw to the airfare for the return flight. We came back to India after a gruelling three months of confinement. It felt good to be back on home ground especially to be able to be close to the family.

Mum was happy to see us. She gave me a welcome home hug I'll never forget. The other good thing was that because of the 'imprisonment', we didn't end up spending too much at all. We found that we had actually managed to save a little money. We had been contemplating the purchase of our own place. Besides, the children needed to be put in school and given a formal education and we had already missed a whole year. I was very sure that I wanted to start settling down to a more normal routine. I knew that we had extended the blissful nomadic lifestyle a little longer than was necessary. Albert was seven and Noella was five when we decided to settle down in India.

Rony was doing a short-term stint but was tired of being at sea and could not bring himself to be away from the family anymore. His thoughts were sealed even more when he called up one evening and I told him that I suspected that I might be expecting a baby – our third. I wanted to share my apprehension with him and to tell him that I wasn't prepared for this unexpected arrival. Mentally, I was quite content with one boy and one girl.

My family was well balanced and I was happy that the children were old enough to do things independently in most respects. Rony was delighted. "Mark my words Milly!" he said. When Albert and Noella get married and go away, this little one is going to be around to keep you young. You just wait and see. This is the best news I've heard in a long time. I always wanted to have a brood of children anyway. I'm thrilled. Don't worry about anything. You're going to be just fine."

He was ever so encouraging that his words soothed me. I felt assured that he was going to be there through this pregnancy and even if I was on the older side, I was hale and hearty enough to give birth to a normal healthy baby.

I accepted it and then I felt a sense of peace. I began looking forward to the arrival of a new life into our home. It was an exciting prospect. Rony meanwhile went full ahead with his research on starting up a consultancy ship chartering service of his own. Over the years, he had come to know many people in the shipping business and he felt that it would be a good idea to get into the shipping industry when it was looking up.

He decided to put in his own hard earned money and his friends joined the venture too. In a couple of months, we began our search for an apartment of our own. We had put Albert into St. Mary's ICSE, a reputable school in Bombay. It had a huge campus and their students excelled in academics, sports and the extracurricular. I had started Noella in a private nursery and later admitted her to St. Anne's High School in Colaba. Both Josephine's daughter and sister's daughter were studying there. So I felt it would be easier for her to adjust. We were staying at Rony's parents' home and would spend time at my mother's place alternatively.

Roslynn at age 3 months at the Holiday Inn, Juhu on a family outing.

On the 8th of May, I was taken to the Hospital. I was nervous about delivering this baby. My gynaecologist, who had delivered both Albert and Noella, was very reassuring.

I had been told about late pregnancies and the dangers involved for both the baby and the mother. Some people had even offered advice, saying that an oxygen mask helps you to calm down and reduces the pain during labour. I remember yelling out to the nurses when I got my first few contractions – "Give me the oxygen mask now!" Dr. Winifred tried to explain that the oxygen mask does not help but I wouldn't take no for an answer. I kept insisting till she relented and ordered the nurses, "Get her the oxygen mask. Maybe then she'll calm down!" The Oxygen mask was promptly thrown aside when the pain was unbearable. I knew then that the doctor was right. It gave me no relief whatsoever. I just concentrated on pushing with all my strength. A couple of minutes later, I was holding an angel in my arms.

The debate started as to what we'd name her. We wanted to name her after her grandparents like we did for Albert, since we couldn't do that for Noella, our Christmas child. There was a slight problem. My mother's first name was Eremitha and Rony's mother's first name was 'Peregrina'. We promptly asked our mothers what their second names were. Thankfully, we liked both. My mum's middle name was Rosalind and Rony's mother's middle name was Anna. So we christened the baby Roslynn Ann Pereira a month later.

Now that our family had grown, I was even more determined to move out on our own. I needed that space and privacy more than ever.

We found an apartment in Bandra West, on a nice hill called Mount Mary's. It was a small place but one we could afford in the given circumstances. Rony said that it was just going to be a stopgap.

Mount Mary's was a beautiful road. At least we had made the right choice in the location. It was bright and breezy with a sea view and a breath-taking view of the sunset in the evenings. It was higher than sea level so it was cooler and the air was fresh and unadulterated; almost pollution free. The compound was large and there were so many children the same age as the kids that they enjoyed going down to play in the evenings. It reminded me of my own childhood and how much fun it was playing in large groups. They'd play 'Cops and Robbers' – we called it 'Chor Police' Bombay style. Noella enjoyed 'Hop-Scotch' with the girls and the skipping rope game. Rony would never miss an opportunity to bowl a few balls himself whenever he passed the playing field. He always encouraged Albert to take part in as many sports and outdoor games as possible. He felt that was the best way for young boys to spend their energy and besides it would keep them out of trouble. 'Clean fun' was what he was all for.

We really liked the neighbours and Rony was glad that I had settled down so well and made friends so easily. They were ever willing to help, were friendly and kind and made my days light-hearted and fun. I remember learning so much from them. Their generosity, openness, whole-hearted love, humility and their service was constant and always with a smile! Such good souls; so Christ-like in every way; living examples. One would make time to help the aged, she'd give of her time and run errands for them herself. I admired her free spirit, her frankness and practicality. She said it like it was! My neighbours thought fondly of me too and I can still recall that the best compliment I have ever received in my life was from them, "You know Milly! If there is ever an earthquake or it's the end of the world or something, we will all come running to your home. Then we know we will be safe. God will allow the whole building to drop around you but your home will stand strong and firm!" Their daughters would always come over before an exam to ask me to pray for them. "When you pray, I'm sure the exam will go well, Aunty!" God taught me the essence of Christianity through these 'Non-Christian' sisters of mine more than any sermon in the church could have! *For the entire law is fulfilled in keeping this one command: "Love your neighbour as yourself." Galatians 5:14*

Anyway, coming back to our choice of a home; for one thing the change in location did wonders for Noella's health. She used to be so sickly at the age of six-seven. She had shed all that lovely baby fat and had become virtually a stick; skin on bone. She had Asthma and very often got respiratory attacks that left her breathless especially in the nights. She had to be propped upright almost to ease the coughing and this helped her stop gasping for breath.

Once, I remember, before we moved to Bandra, Noella had fallen very ill. She had high temperature of 103 degrees and the cold compresses I placed on her forehead didn't seem to work. The fever would just refuse to come down and I was afraid that we would have to admit her to the hospital. That night, Noella awoke from her sleep and began mumbling incomprehensible gibberish, almost like nonsense syllables. She looked terrified and was pointing to the ceiling with a look of horror on her face muttering about big and small bugs. Tears began to roll down her face and I realised she was hallucinating. I woke up Rony and he immediately called the doctor. He prescribed some medicine to bring the fever down immediately and told us that if the fever did not recede in an hour, we would have to admit her. Noella turned worse every second. She was utterly delirious and I was becoming hysterical too. "Do something now! I exclaimed. My baby's dying!

I had begun to sob uncontrollably. Rony as always had to take the matter into his own hands. He held me firmly and said, "We have done what we were told to do. Aren't you the one who keeps telling me to trust in God? Where is that trust now? This child is God's gift to us. We've had her for six years. Surrender her in His hands. If He decides to take her away from us then so be it. Let her go!"

I looked at him incredulously and my expression changed to one of disbelief. "How could he be so merciless!?" I thought. "Is he willing to let our child die?" But his words sunk in and though reluctantly, I said a thanksgiving prayer. "Lord I thank you for this gift of Noella. I surrender her into your hands. Your will be done." But my every thought begged that he would make her well again. No sooner had I made that prayer of surrender, I noticed that Noella's forehead had little beads of sweat. My heart pounded with hope and I reached out and touched her forehead to find that it was cold. She had fallen asleep again. That was one of the 1st signs of His love and I thanked God for showing us His mercy.

So after the bad time, we had with Noella's on-going illness, Florida Apartments, our Bandra home, was a welcome change. The area was less polluted and Noella seemed much better. Signs of Asthma were much less and she seemed happier. She was a very reserved child and preferred just a few select friends. She could spend hours alone, playing with her dolls in an imaginary world. She loved painting and drawing and enjoyed anything creative.

I never had trouble with her studies. She was always self sufficient and very independent. Sometimes too independent. I used to often feel she formed a world around herself and didn't want to be disturbed. It was sometimes difficult to relate to her. If I ever corrected her, she would simply clam up and become expressionless hardly answering any of the questions I raised. It was quite frustrating. She was reticent and wanted to protect herself. She was a very sensitive and defensive child.

Things are very different today. She expresses her love in so many different ways; through her writing, through her support and never fails to tell me how much she loves me whenever she gets the opportunity. I felt disconnected at times but things do change for the better. I think children go through phases and it's our duty to just do the best we can.

Very often, in fact, almost three to four times a day, she would ask me casually, "Mummy do you love me?" When I'd take her in my arms and tell her how much, she'd look happy but not convinced. Invariably that question would come up again and again. "Does mummy treat you badly or differently from Albert or Roslynn?" I used to ask curiously. "No!" she'd reply. "Do you get less love and attention from me?" "No!" she'd respond. "I don't know why, but I just feel you don't like me."

One day, I heard from Josephine that there was this nun called sister Usha who was to come to the Retreat House, which was close by, at the top of Mount Mary hill. She was gifted with a great, divine healing power. She was a simple south Indian nun. I thought it was an excellent opportunity for me to take the children to see her. Albert was suffering from 'Psoriasis' and Noella 'Asthma' – both chronic.

She was known to do an 'Inner healing' which was supposed to get to the root of the problem. She spoke to Noella and asked her many questions about her childhood, about us and our relationship with each other. She asked her what she liked and disliked and what her fears were. She prayed over Noella for twenty minutes and was inspired by the Lord. She asked Noella a very pertinent question and pretty inappropriate for a child I had felt when Noella related the meeting to me. She had asked Noella to ask me whether she was an unwanted child. "Did your mother want a son instead of a girl?" to which Noella responded simply, "No! I'm quite sure she was very happy with a girl because she already had a boy."

I thought hard about that. She had recommended that I think back to the time I conceived Noella. I suddenly got a flashback to the moment I first missed my period and I knew I was pregnant. I had moaned, "Oh! No! Not again…not so quickly! Please let me not be pregnant again!" I enjoyed looking after her. It was such a pleasure. But I guess that initial, instant rejection may have been imbibed subliminally. I spoke to sister Usha about it and she prayed especially for that time in Noella's life. The time of her conception and the rejection she may have experienced while in the womb. She instructed us to say a prayer together and for me to ask Noella's forgiveness so that she could be released from the bondage of rejection. That evening I said that prayer and I sincerely asked Noella's forgiveness. She felt rather awkward but I requested her to take it seriously and accept my apologies. She smiled and caught hold of both my hands. "I forgive, you mummy." She said sweetly. She never had another asthma attack. And Oh yes! She stopped asking me if I loved her repeatedly.

Albert, on the other hand, didn't quite receive the healing I had been praying for. We tried skin specialists and homoeopathic medicine to cure it from the roots. One doctor suggested an elaborate procedure; to make a concoction like an Alternative medicine from 'Ayurvedic' ingredients. Every night before bed, I'd make the paste and apply it on the dry, sore, affected areas on his body, especially on his knees, elbows and tailbone area and carefully tie plastic around those joints. Albert bore all this discomfort and embarrassment silently, never complaining. He had to make sacrifices. He wasn't allowed to go swimming in the sea or in swimming pools although he loved to swim.

I remember once when Fr. Hillary had come over he was happy to see the family and the children. We laughed about how I had gone to him and confided that I was confused about whether or not I should marry or join the convent to be a nun. A lot of people had said that I would make a good one but I wasn't fully convinced. He had asked me what I felt inside when I envisioned it and I had felt a bit apprehensive. He told me categorically that I should get married. "You'll do a lot more good on the outside then you'll do becoming a nun. Marriage is a vocation too! You know? I'm sure you will make some young man very happy too." He said with his wry smile. I remembered how I was so surprised that, being a priest, he still advised me to marry instead.

Albert walked in at that time and he went straight inside. Fr. Hillary asked me if he was shy. I said yes! He asked me if I hugged him often. I was surprised again and said that Albert wasn't too fond of hugs! "He would be embarrassed." I reasoned. He called Albert out and asked him, "Do you like Mummy to hug you?" Albert answered, "I love it!" I was so taken aback by his outburst. Sometimes we mums presume a lot for our kids based on their gender or personality but it's just that; presumptions and stereotypes that may or may not be true at all!

I tried my best to be there for the children as they were growing up. I was curious to know every little detail about their lives. I'd pick a time when they were ready to open up and ask leading questions so they'd get an opportunity to talk about their day, tell me about their friends and teachers, their achievements and their failures. They found a good listening ear in me and I'd simply give them my undivided attention. Sometimes if I was busy, they began tailing me unconsciously from room to room as I went about doing my chores though I was still paying rapt attention. I'd lend my perspective here and there but more often than not I found that they loved being heard and understood. They felt sure that I was 'on their side' and that I wanted to know the truth even if it meant them getting scolded and sometimes if required punished. I made that distinction with them; their actions bore consequences but it didn't mean that I loved them any less. Yes! I was disappointed if they did something they shouldn't have, but I made sure they knew that no matter what, I loved them and that was NEVER going to change.

The girls loved to relate their goings on but Albert was not so talkative. I'd have to prod him to open up. So when he was in a good mood, we'd all take the opportunity to share our stories. The girls loved hearing his opinion and they both looked up to him. He too, though on the quieter side, liked to hear their chatter. As Roslynn grew up, she could talk non-stop and she kept the whole family entertained with her enactments, imitations and stories of her fiery 'come backs'. As she grew up I adopted a different parenting style with her. She was born free as they say. Punishments, denials and admonishments didn't work with her at all. She was short tempered and had boundless energy and often got into trouble. I'd get warnings from my own relatives and friends who believed she would turn into a spoilt brat if she wasn't reprimanded and controlled. One nun even went as far as to call her a 'problem child' and she was deeply hurt by it. It took a lot to undo the impact of those words. Words are powerful and I wish more people in positions of authority could be more sensitive & watch what leaves their mouths more carefully; words can cut deep like a sword and the wounds don't heal without a scar. What is that really?...A 'problem child'; One that doesn't quickly fall in line? Has opinions and questions the way things are? Is confident enough to express them, albeit out of turn; a child who's inclinations might be creative and not academic? I asked myself, as a parent, a teacher and much later as a counsellor too, who are we to decide or label?

Roslynn was quick witted, emotionally intelligent and empathetic and I believed strongly that she responded best to love, encouragement and positive reinforcement. She knew I'd defend her when she felt attacked. She tells me today that the single belief that got her through those rough-edged phases, was that I unequivocally believed that she had it in her to be the bigger and better person, rise up to the challenge of change and evolve with each mistake. She imbibed my advice and would actually go out and face the world with renewed vigour. Watching her grow as a person, address her weaknesses and excel at whatever she did gave me great joy. When significant others expect only the best from you, you tend to feel compelled not to disappoint them and yourself. The positivity is self-fulfilling. I'm glad I went with my instinct with her.

The children all tell me that their friends envied their relationship with me. They were surprised to learn that they shared everything with me; the good, the bad and the ugly! I think what kept the kids on the straight and narrow even in their adolescent years later, was the deep emotional connect we all shared. They so wanted to please and make me proud and couldn't bring themselves to disappoint me. There were times they'd do foolish things, commit mistakes they regretted; I've had to face principals, teachers, parents and once even the police but each time we all came out of those experiences stronger. I had their backs when they'd fall and their trust in the certainty that I was there for them 100% of the way kept them from going astray. I guess they knew deep down inside that nothing else mattered except for each of them. They felt loved and cherished and I feel so grateful and blessed when they now tell me that the assured feeling that they mattered to me so much was what built their self-esteem, their resilience when faced with emotional stress and made them surer of themselves despite peer pressure and the temptations of the big bad world.

I sometimes felt guilty that I'd often sit chatting with my friends in my neighbours flat. We used to have such fun sharing our parenting tips, funny stories and I used to enjoy my neighbour's Idlis, Dosas and hot tea. They made me feel so welcome! They used to call me up to their place quite often – "There's a phone call for you Aunty Milly!" they'd inform me. I confided in Fr. Hillary telling him that I sometimes felt guilty 'wasting' my time like that! He asked me if the time I spent there was interfering with the time I needed to spend with the children or eating into important family matters. I said it wasn't as it was when they were away at school. He assured me that it was time well spent. "Time with friends, laughing, sharing and helping each other grow is good for the soul. As long as you're not gossiping, it's a delightful thing to do! It's not a waste of time at all!" He always cleared doubts I had and made me feel so much better. It reminded me of the wise triple filter test accredited to Socrates. He urged us to ask ourselves three introspective questions when faced with gossip: Is it true? Is it Kind? Is it useful? If it's neither, then why hear it or say it at all?

Parenting is not easy! It's one of THE most important roles we play; It's a calling; a vocation. We learn the psychology of each of our children and deal with them in the way they will best relate. We discipline them with firm unrelenting love 'for their own good' and we persevere though they might rebel, slacken, resent and sometimes even disown from sheer embarrassment, they will eventually realise the heart of a parent in the circle of life.

Train up a child in the way he should go; even when he is old he will not depart from it. - Proverbs 22:6

Chapter 9

Through Thick and Through Thin

In 1980 Rony decided to call it a day from sea life and he joined hands with another Captain to take up ship brokerage.

His business was his life thereafter. He would leave home, drive in our green Ford Cortina, only to return at 11.00 pm on a few good nights otherwise I'd be waiting for him by the window sometimes at 2.00 am and 3.00 am, fuming inside because he hadn't called to say where he would be or what time he was expected back. The life he envisioned for himself; to enjoy life with the family, be there for his kids more, were all being beaten by the incessant demands and relentlessness of a self-owned business venture.

The days we'd hear his cab draw up at a reasonable time, perhaps 9.30 pm or 10.00 pm, the kids, if they were still awake, would all run to the doorway and excitedly wait to jump into his arms as he walked up the flight of stairs.

Trying to manage his business almost single-handedly without much support or input from his partners and burning not only the midnight oil but also a very significant hole in his business coffer, trying to maintain the high living for his employees…..really ate into his capital.

The stress began to get to him. He wasn't very good at dealing with this kind of pressure. He'd tell me all the tales of his woes at the office. Rony took to drinks to soothe his nerves. Eating was also a great stress reliever for him. He loved food. He had a tendency to gain weight, which he did. Oh! How awful those years were!

All we seemed to do was socialise; something I was not comfortable doing in the least. I used to get upset every time he mentioned we had a party to attend or throw. Very often without notice, he'd invite people over and when I would protest saying I hadn't even cooked anything, he would just brush it off saying, "Don't worry about it! We'll order in."

I'd get intimidated with his sophisticated friends with their lovely, lavish homes, their intellectual conversations; their charm and their wit, half their humour would go above my head. How I longed to be home in the comforts of my humble four walls. Those couple of years flew by with nothing but this kind of lifestyle; working, partying, playing snooker at the Willington Gymkhana and gambling away hard earned money. To add to that boozing, smoking, eating out, useless chit chat with friends; A life of excess slowly and insidiously gnawing away at Rony's health. The battering his young body took, out of choice was such a pity and he refused to see reason. Youth is so wasted on the youth.

Meanwhile, Rony also got involved with music; his 1st love and passion. He was asked to do an 'Elvis' segment at a live entertainment production called 'Foot Tapper' in 1982. He was overweight at the time but his velvet voice, which sounded exactly like Elvis if you had your eyes closed and the famous 'Elvis jig' he did to perfection, had rave reviews in local newspapers. They said of his performance, "I saw Capt. Ronnie Pereira in action! Ronnie, used to be Bombay's Elvis at one time! The good Cap'n, who looks like an aging Elvis, did sing like the Pelvis in his prime."

That was a taste of a dream he had forgotten which jogged his memory enough to set him on a simultaneous quest to put up his own entertainment show. I thought he was taking on too much. But with strong hedging from friends, he began lining up artists to perform at his production. He called it 'Ban Dang Boomerang' and had some of the most prominent and promising artists take part.

Again he pumped a lot of his own personal funds into the production as he found it hard to get sponsors, being a newcomer to the entertainment scene. He put his heart and soul into it. After months of preparation, practice sessions that blew a hole in his pocket, he finally raised the curtains on 'Ban Dang Boomerang' at the 'Rang Bhavan' hall in Marine Lines.

He had the likes of a then up and coming singer, Gary Lawyer doing: 'You don't bring me Flowers', he had Sharon Prabhakar performing 'Hot Stuff' and he himself re-created the famous 'Jail-House Rock' scene with a beautiful stage set, jail birds all doing a rhythmically choreographed sequence to the rock-n-roll beats that set the audiences' hearts afire!! He sang 'Teddy Bear', 'Believe Me' and 'That's all right Mama'. He was simply outstanding! The papers said he was 'Spell Binding' and that made all the effort worthwhile.

I was so proud of him and so relieved when it was all over. He got rave reviews and everyone that saw his show wanted him to put up a sequel but he was just happy that he had managed to pull it all together in the end. He barely covered his costs.

To celebrate the success of the show and to take a break from the hard work they had all put in, we took off with family friends to Uduwada and Ooty. We hired some cars with drivers and hit the road. The countryside was spectacular. The kids were so excited.

Our reverie turned to horror when our driver who might have dozed off for a second, awoke with a start and lost control of the car, trying to swerve away from an oncoming vehicle. In seconds, we were flying off the road. Our mid air flight seemed to be in slow motion and we hit the ground with such a powerful impact that the driver got thrown from the car as the door swung open. I cried out, "Jesus!" The Lord's hand was upon us, unbelievably we came away shaken but with just a few scratches, literally! Every day I make it a point to pray for the safety of each one of my family members. Having an accident is one my worst fears and God yet again put his protective mantle over us that fateful day. I thanked and praised him that he had taken care of us and we came away unscathed. We could all have been killed. Rony was so grateful too.

His attention diverted for months, Rony wasn't able to give his business his full, undivided attention. His funds were depleting, as he had not brought in new business. His nerves were rankled. That was the beginning of the end for not only his business operations but also for his friendships and partnerships. The months that followed were unbearable for him in many ways. He had huge fallouts with trusted people.

All this stress played havoc both mentally and physically for Ron. Much that it pained his heart, he cut his losses and decided to hang up his businessman's hat. He had to declare bankruptcy and settle so many dues, execute numerous closures and take care of myriad formalities.

I understood our marriage vows better when we went through that rough patch; 'Through thick and through thin' Boy! That was one ultra thin period for us! Hardly any money to barely run the home, Rony was at rock bottom. He had debts to repay. His financial situation was in the doldrums and some of his friendships were over. He felt like a huge failure and we were his only solace.

One morning, he felt very uneasy. He began to sweat and felt a pain in his abdomen and chest. At first, he thought it was gas so he took a tablet to relieve the uneasiness. But it persisted.

We went to see the doctor. The heart specialist made him do an ECG and a stress test. He was baffled with the result. He came out with an expression of utter shock and amazement. "Mr. Pereira would you like to talk alone?" He said tentatively. Rony assured him he could speak in front of me. So the doctor proceeded to explain, "You've suffered a heart attack. I am in shock that you managed to come here and are actually sitting there after what I have seen on your cardiogram." He was immediately admitted to the ICU. He said, "The only reason you're not dead is because your heart is young. It has suffered a huge blow." Cardio infarction is what they called it.

I was so afraid, but I had made a lot of progress in my spirituality and my strengthened faith in the Lord held me together. I would have been a wreck if it weren't for the grace I was obviously showered with from above. I was actually able to give Rony a lot of strength and comfort in his time of need. He had also begun to appreciate my transformation; from an incessant worrier like my father to a peaceful, happier person with implicit trust in Jesus' power and Love. He had even jokingly asked me if I still cared for him as I had begun to sleep peacefully, without waiting up for him.

My frowning face and the silent treatment I'd give him so often was a thing of the past. I would not hassle him or get upset if he came late or went out with his friends without informing me. I didn't keep pestering him to give up smoking and drinking; I simply just got off his case but kept praying for him, lifting up my anxieties to the Lord.

We were more peaceful now in a home that had been sometimes pretty fraught with our arguments, my whining and crying and my swollen eyes, which had become a customary sight for the kids the morning after our frequent spats. I used to hold my ground and very rarely found it in my heart to forgive hurts. I would let my pride get the better of me and I found that the more I fanned my ego, the more difficult our relationship would get. Rony would argue and argue till I'd clam up and allow the tears to flow. He would sometimes get so frustrated with me saying, "You cry at the drop of a hat! Can't we just have a decent conversation without you breaking into tears for a change?" Our fights were affecting the kids too.

One day, I remember walking off in a huff promising never to come back. It was pretty late probably after 9:00 pm and Rony quickly sent Albert after me. He ran behind me and managed to catch up on the Mount Mary steps. I recall crying and telling Albert that his dad did not love me anymore and that I didn't want to come back home ever again. I had let my emotions rule my wisdom and behaved worse than an immature child.

The irony is that while we think we're adults and it seems so on the outside, in actuality, we're all fighting our own battles of the ego and are children on the inside with the same need and yearning for love, acceptance, tenderness and belonging. Instead of giving each other what we need, we let our egos rule and our actions become defiant, rebellious, disrespectful and childish.

The poor children always get dragged into adult battles and more often than not think it is their fault. I thought I could change Rony by telling him to change and by showing my disappointment and anger but when I joined the cell group, soon after Roslynn was born, I slowly learnt that acceptance, love and positivity are the keys that lead to change. I gradually received true grace when I decided to be humble. I began opening my heart and mind to share my fears, my weaknesses and my strengths with my sisters in prayer and I found a huge release after this whole-hearted, genuine surrender; a place for forgiveness and healing.

I very recently received a whatsapp forward and love this excerpt from what Pope Francis said in his homily on the importance of forgiveness in the family, *"There is no perfect family. We have no perfect parents, we are not perfect, do not get married to a perfect person, neither do we have perfect children. We have complaints about each other. We are disappointed by one another. Therefore, there is no healthy marriage or healthy family without the exercise of forgiveness. Forgiveness is vital to our emotional health and spiritual survival. Without forgiveness, the family becomes a theatre of conflict and a bastion of grievances. Without forgiveness, the family becomes sick. Forgiveness is the sterilisation of the soul, cleansing the mind and the liberation of the heart. Anyone who does not forgive has no peace of soul and communion with God. Pain is a poison that intoxicates and kills. Maintaining a wound of the heart is a self-destructive action. It is an autophagy. He who does not forgive sickens physically, emotionally and spiritually. That is why the family must be a place of life and not of death; an enclave of cure not of disease; a stage of forgiveness and not of guilt. Forgiveness brings joy where sorrow produced pain; and healing, where pain caused disease."*

I recall how Eric and Jo introduced me to the charismatic movement soon after I got married. I attended their praise and worship sessions and I used to be embarrassed raising my hands to praise God. I was inhibited, always looking around to see what people might think of me. I was proud and felt it was silly to throw my hands up or talk in tongues like some others were 'blessed' to do. I listened to their 'gibberish' and their nonsense syllables and it often amused me. I have to admit feeling sorry for my mum and the whole family who seemed to have got caught up in a cult of sorts and I was actually worried that they would be swayed away from the Church.

After many years of continuously attending the cell and prayer group meet ups and following the path, witnessing the praise and worship sessions, reading the word of God, I slowly began understanding the abandonment and devotion with which they worshipped the good Lord.

They died to their bodily forms and sang with their souls uplifted with nothing but gratitude and praise; not praying for something from a selfish place but with unconditional glorification and I knew in my heart of hearts that the Lord was pleased. I went for a retreat to give thanks. My mum came over to help out and I was away for just a few days, close at hand and would drop by for a few minutes each morning to make sure everyone was ok. I remember still not being very comfortable with the praise and worship sessions; with raising my hands and being overt in my praise. I had always preferred to do it silently, in my mind.

One morning at the chapel, there were sharing sessions and many others were going up to the podium to give their testimonies. They were proclaiming his name for healings received and miracles in their lives. I didn't have a single thing to share and was praying quietly, giving thanks to God for my family and the love I received from them. Suddenly, out of the blue, I started to feel a shiver enter my spine. I began shaking from head to toe and didn't know what had overcome me! The whole bench began to shake and I couldn't help it. Part of me was embarrassed but I simply had no control over it, much as I tried to calm myself down. Suddenly I found myself getting up and walking via the aisle towards the podium. I was beyond myself!

It was like a dream I had no control over where I saw myself doing things I would never do in reality except this was no dream – It was as real as it got! I took the microphone and words left my mouth before I had had time to think of them myself. I felt I was led by the Holy Spirit, "I praise and thank Jesus that I was once shy and could never bring myself to worship publicly with my hands raised and now I can!! Praise God!! Amen!"

That was all I said; my first ever, public testimony. I walked back in a daze, cringing at the absolute fool I had just made out of myself. Later that night, I tossed and turned going over what I had done. How silly I felt! One line! That too nothing really miraculous at all, like the others had related. The next morning at breakfast, I had a few people come up, tap me and tell me what an excellent testimony I had given! It was the affirmation I needed. I realised it was a greater force that compelled me to act and to proclaim my internal victory with my tongue – It was the beginning of my journey in my metamorphosis from a shy, introverted caterpillar to a butterfly, colourful in spirit, stronger in faith and being readied to take flight!

Very recently, when I attended an inner-healing retreat in Kerela, down south. I met a devout nun who spent time with each of us to heal us of past hurts in our lives. She prayed with me silently and after a few minutes, she told me that she had had a vision of a young girl standing outside a charismatic renewal centre with a frown on her face and her hands crossed. She didn't know who the girl was or what the vision meant for me. She asked that I go to the chapel to reflect on that vision to decipher through God's wisdom, what it might mean for my healing.

I was initially baffled, as it didn't connect immediately. But when I meditated upon that imagery I began to understand what God was trying to convey to me. I fought with the thoughts that pervaded my mind. "But I'm fully convinced, Lord! I am completely involved in your charismatic work and I have been following your will for so long now. Have you not forgiven me for being that young girl frowning outside the church? I'm no longer that person!" I immediately received the answer I was looking for, "You have not asked for forgiveness for that yet. You looked down upon my work and my people and were haughty enough to stand outside in judgement." I begged for forgiveness that day and it was a healing I didn't even know I needed!

A lot of us Christians often wonder whether 'confession' is really necessary; most of us do it because we have to. But I realised through this incident that our sin is in believing we are sinless; that we don't need forgiveness for anything, after all, we do what is expected of us; follow the directives of the Church, pray, do good deeds, give to charity and don't do anything wrong like robbing, lying, cheating etc. Jesus is a forgiving God but I realised that I needed to seek his forgiveness before I could receive it. If we stand outside the door with a frown like I had, thinking no end of myself; that I was righteous and didn't need to be forgiven, then we stay right there, outside the pearly gates, shocked that He isn't letting us inside.

A few months after I joined the prayer group, I developed a severe case of cervical spondylitis. It had started with a severe neck ache, a shooting pain that would extend all the way to my arms. I'd get spasms. I could not lift my hands beyond eye level so putting on T-shirts and blouses without buttons became a real task for me. I would spend more than half an hour in the bathroom trying to clothe myself and would cry with frustration. Eventually, I'd stick to only button down or very loose blouses that were easier to put on and take off. I had been prescribed the neck belt and medicines to relieve the pain.

The tractions I had done were of no help and I was told that only prolonged exercises would relieve the condition over time; there was no real cure. I shared my woes with my cell group. Our group leader, Doreen suggested that we all pray together for my healing. So they all placed their hands on me and prayed earnestly that I make a full recovery. I recall feeling the weight of their hands and how unbearable the pain was! I was praying for them to finish quickly so I could be relieved of the weight!

I felt so guilty to be distracted and so unfaithful! But I obediently claimed as I was instructed, "I believe Lord that you have healed me. I claim your healing in Jesus' name. By your stripes and wounds, I am healed!" Not I *will* be healed or *Please heal me* but to claim that I have *already* received healing.

Everyone would keep enquiring whether I felt any relief. They also prayed for a miracle. I have to admit that doubts crossed my mind but each time I would cast them aside and claim a healing with fresh vigour and faith. Four days later, I noticed that I was able to raise my arms to point towards the ceiling without wincing in pain.

I praised God and I couldn't wait to share the good news with my sisters at the cell group. They were equally excited and we all just praised Jesus' name that day from beginning to end. I claimed that complete cure and I believed he wanted to show me His mercy so that I would believe. As we were praying and worshipping and giving thanks for His miracle, the pain suddenly returned and with a new vengeance! It was worse than ever before this time! I winced but tried to hold it together as I didn't want to shatter the ladies' faith and be a dampener.

While walking home that day, I burst out to one of the ladies accompanying me home. "The pain is back. It's worse than ever! I can't help it! I don't know what to do and I feel awful to break it to you. Please don't tell the others. I don't want them to feel bad!" She had newly joined the prayer group and even so, she was used as an instrument in that moment. She turned around and stopped in her tracks! "Milly! This is a test! Stay strong and continue to claim your healing! We all will! You need the support of our sisters more than ever now!!" I found it hard to keep claiming His healing but I did it nonetheless! The pain persisted for a week and it was the toughest test to continue to believe through the pain!

Doreen was a Godsend. She would come over with tasty cutlets and chicken curry because I couldn't lift a finger in the house. She would go out of her way to be of service. Very often she would be guided by His will to act upon thoughts that entered her mind while she meditated and prayed. I admired her connection with the Lord. She was so committed, disciplined and compassionate. I thanked God for the friend she had become; one of my dearest and closest confidantes and to think it was the same woman I'd felt intimidated to hold a conversation with in the past.

I questioned God and his motives. "Why? Lord!" I pleaded. I had surrendered to you and believed you had worked this miracle in my life and now you take it all back. Why are you testing my faith?" I was so ashamed to call Doreen and let her know of my predicament. I felt so foolish after all the claiming and praising I had made them all do the day before. She just filled me with renewed hope. "Don't let the evil one make you believe anything else. He is testing your faith and God sometimes allows it. Even Jesus was tested. Claim this healing as your own. Know that God loves you and has healed you." She said firmly. I began to pray and claim. The pain would return in spasms and each time I would claim His healing and praise Him and thank Him in advance for the healing. This went on for a week and every day I would believe and claim, till one day the pain just vanished.

I had been shown God's mercy and His infinite love and I believed more than ever before that he was working His miracles through His Holy Spirit in our everyday lives and those that felt he only worked miracles in the Biblical era were wrong. He is alive among us and wants us all to let him in. I was his Doubting Thomas, converted.

The doctors had told me I would have to live with it and that there was no cure. I wanted to praise Jesus! And sing from the mountains as he had made the impossible possible!! Rony was also overjoyed to hear the news of my recovery....so too Eric and Jo and my kids who were all so happy for me. I shared my testimony with so many women thereafter.

There was a neighbour in my building, who came over to my place one day and shared with me that she had developed cancer and asked me to pray for her. My heart went out to her. I knew I couldn't begin to understand her pain and suffering but I so wanted to comfort her. I was unsure of how she would react to my spondylitis story but I felt prompted to tell her anyway. The intention was to relate my victory in Faith. I asked her to claim His healing and to continue to trust.

She was very inspired by my testimony and went about claiming a healing just like I had done so many years before. Except she wasn't coy about it like I was; claiming healing quietly in my mind, feeling silly as I struggled through the pain and yet kept repeating, "I am healed!!" She went around loudly proclaiming it to everyone she met. "I am a cancer patient! But I have full faith that I am being healed by Jesus!" Her faith was unrelenting.

She would go for her chemotherapy with determination and even as her hair fell off and she moved around with a scarf, completely bald, looking wan, pale and weak, she would have a smile on her face and praise God for His healing. Today, she is hale and hearty, travelling abroad and back to stay with her daughter and son who have settled there for good. She continues to testify of His miracle in her life and is always grateful to me for sharing my story of faith. "I am a cancer survivor!" is now her happy introduction.

So when I saw Rony lying there helpless, all hooked up to tubes and monitors, I prayed for his complete recovery as well. I prayed that Rony would be given a new heart. I had a testimony to remind him of and Rony too began turning to the Lord in his darkest hours. He asked for five more years. "I realise now the folly of my ways, Milly." He said to me. I have brought this on myself with my life of excess. If God grants me just five years, I will live right and set things right, the way I had planned. I lost sight of that plan and I have learnt the hard way." I encouraged him to surrender himself and his condition to the Lord and to ask for his heart to be healed. I kept telling him that he would be healed completely!

We left the hospital with a final ECG. The specialist was surprised. He showed us the first ECGs in comparison. "There is no sign of a scar or blemish on your heart. It's as good as new!" He exclaimed. Normally the signs of a previous heart attack would never just disappear like that. They were as astounded as we were. We looked at each other with joyous smiles on our faces. The good Lord was good indeed!

He replied, "Because you have so little faith. Truly I tell you, if you have faith as small as a mustard seed, you can say to this mountain, 'Move from here to there,' and it will move. Nothing will be impossible for you." – Mathew 17:20

For by grace you have been saved through faith. And this is not your own doing; it is the gift of God, not a result of works, so that no one may boast. - Ephesians 2:8-9

Chapter 10

Turning Over a New Leaf

A week later, Rony left the hospital a new man. He walked out hale and hearty in more ways than one. Praise God! He had worked yet another miracle and we thanked him from the bottom of our hearts.

Rony was true to his word or his end of the bargain he had made with God. He gave up smoking. He gave up drinking and went on a strict diet of soups, vegetables and occasionally fish or chicken. He started an exercise regime and was so disciplined. I was amazed at his will power. He was a transformed man.

His eldest brother had lent him money to get by during this difficult time. He was determined to pay back every dime. Eric too lent as much as he could. Rony felt it was high time he returned to the high seas. But he wanted to be sure he was fit to take on a seafaring job after his heart attack.

He was a bit apprehensive about the mandatory medical tests required prior to joining the ship. He applied for a job and was asked to do his medicals, which thankfully showed no traces of his previous heart attack. Rony landed a job with a very good company on a very sturdy ship. He found the run easy too; six months on and three months off. He resisted the urge to have us flown down to join him this time. He was determined to fill the empty coffers again. He would make sure he continued his rigorous walks on board, striding up and down the deck. He had instructed the cook to prepare special meals for him and he just determinedly stuck to healthy food. He was half his size when I saw him next. I told him jokingly, "You look so young, people might ask me if you're my son now!" He laughed. He was happy with his progress and I was so proud of his courage and determination.

If only he had been able to lead a disciplined life like this much earlier; things would have been very different. He began repaying his brother. He would send money to him periodically. Things got better slowly. After a couple of years at sea, once he had built up some capital and repaid most of his debts, he couldn't hold on any longer. He promised the kids that if they fare well in their exams he would send for them and they could have a very long two months holiday on board with him. They were so excited! He landed in Bangkok, Thailand and he invited Eric and Jo to join us as well with their whole family. He went all out to show them a good time. It was a fantastic vacation with the whole extended family.

We created some memories to last a lifetime. That was what Ron believed in. Living life to the fullest and enjoying the opportunities whenever possible. He was never one to think of saving for a rainy day and he found it very difficult to really curb himself from spending. In hindsight, I guess we cherish the unforgettable memories more than any money he may have left behind.

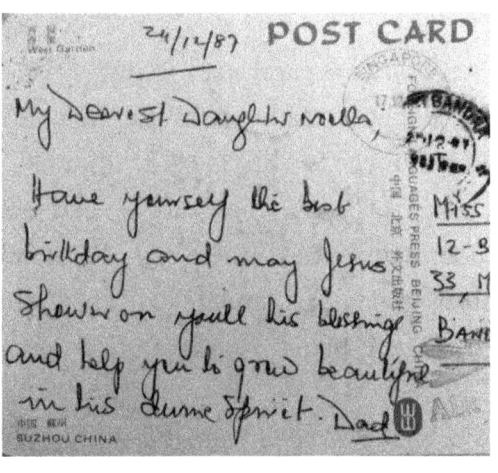

Postcard from Rony to Noella in 1987 with blessings that I felt so happy to read!

Rony's letters to the children were full of advice. He hated being away from them at a crucial time in their lives when he felt that Noella and

Albert were turning into adolescents and needed to be guided more than ever. He wrote beautiful letters to both of them on how they would experience changes in their bodies and how it meant that they were soon going to become adults and how they could become responsible ones with heads firmly on their shoulders.

He didn't leave Roslynn out. He'd address her so lovingly, "My dearest Lil' Loll" and ask about her friends, her performances and her studies. They had a unique equation. He doted on her, encouraged her sprightliness and was amused when she behaved like her usual 'drama queen'. He indulged her many quirks allowing her natural personality to bloom influencing her creativity with his made-up stories of adventurous, imaginative, curious, fearless and strong-minded girls; 'Susie & Prudence'. He'd compose poems for her birthday and sometimes allow her to celebrate it multiple times a year even!

Writing always came easy to him. I felt I couldn't write letters well and I loved that he made up for me. He made sure to make his presence felt and build a bond with his kids from half way across the world. He kept in touch with his whole family that way; mine included, all over the globe. Family ties were very important to him. He loved people and valued bonds. His letters also began with words like, "Pray every day. Jesus loves you."

I knew he was accepting Him more and more in his life and it gave me immense joy that he was finding the Lord. A man who used to stand outside the church, if he came at all; a man who was indifferent. He never liked rituals or must-dos. He would write to me telling me how the Lord had worked wonders in his dealings with difficult agents and with port authorities and how with a little prayer to the almighty things would turn around so remarkably. I praised God when I read those lines. I knew Rony was in the best hands. When he was in Bombay, he began coming to church every Sunday and helping the kids to make it on time. He would come into the church and sit down with all of us, explaining to me when I expressed my happiness at his sea change, "I have to be an example to the kids. I can't just tell them to go inside. That doesn't work."

I recall the days when this was a dream for me and how because it never happened it used to infuriate me. I'd wake up early and remind Rony several times so we could be ready for church on time but he'd just nod in agreement and continue to watch the TV or read his newspaper.

I was annoyed, seeing how flippant he was when it came to church. The least he could do was be an example to the children and if he respected my wishes he would at least make an effort! I felt he didn't care for me because he never seemed to care and he knew how important it was to me! I hated being late or having to stand outside with the kids in tow. After the mass, he'd have the gall to suggest we take the kids out or meet up with some friends and I was so mad, I'd refuse to fall in with his plans because he refused to cooperate with mine!

My pride would convert that Sunday into a Black Sunday with my black face and black, unforgiving heart instead of a Holy, happy Sunday like I wanted it to be. That was the biggest irony and my own failings, my impatience and judgmental attitude spoilt it for us all.

The renewal, the prayer group, the sharing, helped me in a big way to change not only my husband like I wanted to but to transform my own heart. The Lord spoke to me and I realised that I had to let go! To become a good wife was to accept and my husband with his faults and to love him despite them! I prayed for forgiveness for my self-righteousness and slowly but surely I was given the grace to begin to accept and love unconditionally. I tried it reluctantly. I had to hold back my mood, the many taunting things I wanted to say. I told the Lord how difficult it was to love someone who wasn't even willing to love God!

I was asking him to come to church after all! It was a battle going on inside of me. It was hard as the worry would get the better of me sometimes, especially during the days he'd smoke or drink socially. "I can hold my drinks well" would be his excuse to drink excessively and how I would seethe!

I began accepting him and his vices. One day, I even offered to light his cigarette and he was taken aback at my audaciousness. "You've started smoking!?" He asked incredulously and I said, "I want to help you light one up, that's all!" I lit it in my mouth and gave it to him. I felt a sense of freedom in that moment.

I had surrendered my battle to the Lord and had received His grace to genuinely let go that which I couldn't control. ***He*** was going to handle Rony's addictions.

During that phase, one day he had gone out to the balcony to have a smoke. He either left the home or would duck out for a quick puff as he didn't want to smoke in front of the children or me, knowing that passive smoking was equally bad for health. Suddenly, out of the blue, he came inside and said decidedly, "Milly, I've decided I'm going to kick the habit!" He snuffed the cigarette he had lit and proclaimed that it was his last. I was taken aback! True to his word he never touched another cigarette.

I had stopped nagging him. I began waiting for him patiently, without getting bugged much as I hated going to church late. I thought of my image and what people would think of me walking in late every Sunday. But the Sundays had slowly turned around and we were all much happier. The transformation was for me!

God showed me how I could change my heart and a situation. Rony was eventually the one to nudge the kids into getting ready on time and it felt so good to finally sit inside the church as a whole family, in the front rows.

Rony's heart attack was a kind of wake up call and after the tough phase, it was incredible to connect again and for us to be centred together in God. It was a fantastic time in our relationship and as a family in every way. Second chances are amazing if you use that time to heal the wounds of the past, address your weaknesses and do it right the second time around. Small dreams, BIG achievements in the Lord Jesus!

"Do not be conformed to this world, but be transformed by the renewal of your mind, that by testing you may discern what is the will of God, what is good and acceptable and perfect." – Romans 12:2

Chapter 11

Dreams Do Come True

The following year, he again could not resist the temptation to fly us down for a holiday. This time he said he would be docking in Rio De Janeiro, Brazil and he wanted us to join him before the school holidays began as he would be docked there for a short period of time and would head for Tunisia thereafter.

So I had to get special permission from the schools, especially since the exams were going on and they would miss two test papers. I hated the thought of approaching their principals. I prayed that they grant permission without too much of a hassle. It turned out, both Albert's and the girls' principals were open-minded and progressive.

"By all means, Mrs. Pereira take the kids travelling; that kind of education is an opportunity they'll never get in a classroom." We were so grateful and Noella was ecstatic that she didn't have to study for her Hindi paper. Getting the visas was the next hurdle. They asked for the letters from the agent and the shipping company. They required the airline ticket. I didn't have either of these.

I read their board which said that the minimum application process period was one week. I was there on a Friday with the weekend coming up.

Naturally, the officer there refused and I was walking away when he suddenly called me back and asked for my passports. I was surprised! An hour later, all the passports were stamped with the visas we required. I was so astounded and ever so grateful.

I knew Rony would get a limited time at the port and sail off in two to three days time so timing was everything! If we weren't able to leave immediately, we'd miss the holidays, as the next port he was to dock in, would have been around 2 months later.

I was grateful for his empathy. I praised God for working his wonders through this kind man. I rushed off to get the air tickets and they also couldn't believe that I had managed to get the visas without any wait whatsoever! "It's virtually impossible Mrs. Pereira! How did you do it? Do you have a God Father there at the office?" I laughed excitedly and said, "I have a God! Yes! And he is my father!!"

Off we went on a 23-hour journey to reach 'Paranaguay'. We took a flight from Bombay to Germany, Germany to New York, New York to Rio de Janeiro and on our descent, we saw the magnificent statue of Christ, from the plane. It was stunning. When we reached, we were taken by boat on board the 'M.V Taiho'; an orange bulk carrier, the biggest ship Rony had ever served as Captain.

The kids were so impressed that their daddy was Captain of this magnificent vessel as Rony called her.

The kids were ecstatic. They were really quite grateful. They had learnt that demanding anything didn't get them what they wanted. They accepted that we were tight on money. I used to run the home with a small budget and taught them the value of money right from the start. So anything we gave them as incentives as a surprise, were truly enjoyed and appreciated that much more.

While in Tunisia, we made the decision to send Albert back home in time for the start of his new semester in the 10th grade so that he could attend the pre-tuitions we had enrolled him for and he could put his mind to his studies. He was very mature about it and agreed quite readily even though it meant missing out on a holiday to the United States of America; the kids always dreamed of going there because of their exposure to American media.

America was always portrayed as the land of dreams. You didn't see that kind of modernity anywhere in India so going abroad was a huge deal and only the rich could afford it. We were not rich but earned more than the average middle-class Indian. Rony earning in US dollars made a big difference. But because he believed in spending the money he earned, there was never very much in the bank.

So Albert very bravely and determinedly went back to India all alone.

We carried on to Portland Maine and enjoyed our trip. We tearfully said goodbye to Rony when the holiday came to an end. We had had such a superb time and spent so much quality time together as a family. I used to feel the pinch when he shared with me how much he'd end up spending on these trips but each time I'd exclaim, he would remind me that the kids would be grown in no time and begin their own lives. These were the times I would cherish and no amount of money could replace a lifetime of precious memories.

On returning home, Noella had to write her unit tests almost immediately. She hadn't been present for the lessons for almost two whole months in the eighth grade. She had a lot to catch up on. The teachers were expecting her to fail in most of the subjects but to their amazement she passed in every subject except Hindi, which she had always been weak.

Albert took his tenth grade studies rather casually despite my repeated reminders of how important the year was as a stepping-stone going forward. Passing out of the 10th grade with flying colours would enable him to make life choices thereafter. He knew how much of an impact his grades could have. The best colleges only accepted the best of the best. He would be competing with the SSC board, which was known to turn out top rankers.

He wanted to get into a reputable college and those with a low percentage had to simply take what they got and be grateful that they were given a seat; a predicament he was dreaded being in. So I was surprised that he didn't apply himself in his 1st semester at all. We had sent him back to attend school on time so that he didn't fall back on his studies in any way. We were quite determined to support him in his endeavour to do well in his board exams. But his results were so disappointing.

I was concerned. I asked him if he needed more help, perhaps additional tuitions. I wrote to Ron about his poor performance and he too was worried. "He's lacking confidence that's all! He's giving up before he has given himself the chance to start." Rony said. Two months later Rony came down and stayed at home for 6 months so that he could boost Albert's self confidence.

He drew up a schedule that they followed stringently. Albert was so grateful that Rony had shown so much interest. He did a 360-degree turnaround. He would forgo his evening playtime and football matches to study. Rony would sit with him and they would go through subjects, completing chapter after chapter; ticking them away on the chart, which began to look better and better as the months progressed.

His third term unit tests were much better. He scored higher marks but he was still way short of the percentage Rony wanted and knew he could achieve. Just before his final term papers, Rony had to go back. But he filled Albert with renewed vigour to go at the exams like it was the 1st hurdle he would face in his life's race to the finish line. He told him of his own struggle to make it; to earn well so that he could support his family.

He gave him so many examples of his school mates who just whiled away their time and ended up on the streets as drunks. "You've got to think big and way into the future. How do you see yourself five years from now? Ten years from now? Your actions today will determine whether those visions can be accomplished. I know you have the capability to far exceed your own expectations. All you have to do is believe it yourself and work really hard to achieve it."

This encouragement and the huge effort and faith his dad had put in him spurred Albert on. He seemed more determined than ever to prove himself. He so wanted to make his dad proud. Rony also dangled a carrot just before he left for the airport. "Get me a distinction and you can join me on my next run in Malaysia - just the two us." Albert was so happy and excited with that thought. He worked hard the remaining few months. He managed to complete the whole syllabus and even revise all the chapters before writing his papers. Something he had never done before. We left the rest to God.

Receiving his results two months later was one of the most exciting experiences for us all. Albert had scored 71% in his ICSE Board exams. Colleges at that time equated it with a 76% in a conventional SSC board exam. Rony was overjoyed when he heard the news.

That summer was fabulous for Albert. Shortly after his admissions to H.R College of Commerce, he left for his holiday to join Rony in Kuala Lumpur Malaysia. He was ecstatic and on top of the world! A thrilling place to be when you're his age with the wind in your hair, the spirit of youth and the sheer elation that he had given his dad the opportunity to keep his promise.

I was so happy that they would spend that time together. I knew that a boy his age missed having his father around to discuss everyday events; both good and bad. I felt sure that this time away from all of us girls would be great for the two of them. One would get to relive his boyhood and the other would learn what it was to be a man.

"Or what man is there among you who, when his son asks for a loaf, will give him a stone? "Or if he asks for a fish, he will not give him a snake, will he? "If you then, being evil, know how to give good gifts to your children, how much more will your Father who is in heaven give what is good to those who ask Him! – Mathew 7:9-11

Chapter 12

Life's Unexpected Twists And Turns

Albert wrote home. "I'm having a great time. Malaysia is super. Have already bought football shorts and sports shoes. The food is very good." Rony took him out whenever he could but he was busy a lot of the time so Albert would venture out on his own exploring the streets of Malaysia, the Petronas towers and their theme parks.

I heard the phone ringing very early one morning as if it was in my dream. But it got progressively louder as I awoke from a deep sleep to stagger out of bed, running to reach the phone on time. I wondered who could be ringing that early in the morning. It wasn't even 6.00 am yet. It was still kind of dark, so I fumbled to find the phone. "Hello!" I said hesitantly. "Hi, Mum!" It was Albert. I was so surprised to hear his voice. "Albert? How come you called this early? Is everything all right?" "Not really. Dad is not too well. He's OK, so don't get worried but he's been admitted to the hospital for monitoring and has asked me to tell you to fly down if you can." "What?!!" I blurted out, almost jumping out of the chair. "What's wrong with him?" I was alarmed and I couldn't help worry and think of the worst. At once I thought of the Lord and asked for his grace to calm me down so I could think clearly. Instantly I felt his peace. I told Albert calmly to take care of his daddy till I got there and I called Eric to make arrangements to fly down to Malaysia as soon as was possible.

All the way, I prayed and I requested Doreen, Ralph and Eric and Jo to keep lifting him up in prayer so that he would be all right. I didn't know the condition he was in. Albert mentioned that he had felt uneasy on the ship while on the bridge; just after climbing the stairs to get up to it and he couldn't breathe too well. So he told his chief officer to take charge and with Albert's help, they left for the hospital where they were monitoring his condition. It sounded all too familiar. It was his heart playing up again. "No! Lord" I pleaded with him. "Please make him well again. You did it once before you can do it again."

A day later, when I reached there, I took a cab to the hospital to find Rony and Albert in a normal ward. Rony was sleeping on the bed and Albert was sitting by his side. There was a tube in his nose and it didn't look right at all. I took one look at Rony's face and I knew he was up to something. There was that familiar wry crease of a smile, ever so small, but there.

I walked straight up to him and pulled out the tube from his nose. "The Lord has healed you. This is not what he promised me." I said defiantly. Rony and Albert laughed but he was shocked that I would do something so risky. "What if I really needed that tube? You could have killed me!" He said threateningly. I realised I had been foolish and taken a chance but I felt so sure they were pulling a fast one on me. "How are you?" What are the doctors saying? I want to hear good news." I said confidently. "You're some woman of faith, Milly. That's why I told Albert that I wanted you here by my side. Your positive spirit and your prayers always work wonders."

"_**He**_ works wonders, Ron." I reminded him. He has shown you his love before and he wants to show you again." "The doctors have said that I am making good progress. I had a minor setback on the ship. I need to rest and be away from stress and take it easy. I won't be able to join back; no climbing stairs or lifting heavy things for me for a while. My heart is weak." Rony filled me in.

We prayed that day and every day Rony progressively got better. They had picked up a new colour video camera and he was back to his old joking ways, laughing and kidding around. He had the knack of making light of the most difficult and stressful situations. He took some videos of my embarrassed face and Albert took some clips of Rony singing a few classic songs like 'Evergreen' and 'Green Fields'.

A week later, the doctors said he was fit enough to travel and we praised the Lord for answering our prayers.

We booked our tickets and all flew back home with strict instructions for Rony to take it very easy. He had to recuperate or else he could be very susceptible and vulnerable. His company gave him his release papers and paid for everything without any trouble whatsoever, which he was grateful for.

He expressed how happy he was that Albert was around when he needed family the most. He was a rock and he praised him for helping out at such a crucial time. Albert too was happy that he could be there for his dad.

In the weeks that followed, Rony stayed put at home. He would read his favourite 'Time' magazine and several sports weeklies. He'd read the newspaper from end to end. He also kept reading books on heart disease. At some level his knowledge on the subject made him worry more, I feel. On the face of it, he would seem to be in a good mood always playing around and joking with the kids but he was actually quite worried about his condition.

A fortnight later, Rony decided, on the doctor's advice, that he should admit himself into Hinduja Hospital in Mahim to have a series of extensive tests done. The hospital was top of the line for the time. It had a magnificent view of the Indian Ocean, on the 20th floor; the air-conditioned room was spacious, airy and bright.

The hospital staff were professional and attentive. The lobby was so swanky it gave the hospital the feel of a hotel. Rony would answer calls from friends with a "Hi! Hinduja Hotel! How may I help you?" They would be pleasantly surprised at his propensity to joke around even in the midst of such serious situations. He'd befriend the nurses and charm the ward boys. He'd take the time to find out about their lives and make them laugh. He always got special treatment in hospitals and when he was discharged, they'd all come over to bid him farewell.

Rony was on bland food; soups and salads. He was at home and spent his time relaxing, reading and playing his guitar. I loved the time we spent together. He would join me for evening mass and spent time with the kids, engaging in their daily activities. He had started reading the bible, praying together and it gave me immense joy to see his gradual transformation.

His friend Ralph would dedicatedly come over to share the word from the Bible and they would discuss their perspectives, the nuances from the word and how each scripture would take on a new meaning with a whole new insight every time they read it afresh. It was like an incepted thought God planted for the day. This constant support gave Rony some much needed, peace of mind. It brought a sense of equilibrium to him. He slowly but surely sought out the Bible and God's word started becoming fodder for his soul. It is true that you can take a horse to a lake but you can never force him to drink unless he wants to.

I had tried my hand at 'shepherding' him before but it was always met with a casual undertone like he was humouring me which sort of beat the very purpose. I was filled with joy to see him seek out the Lord, make Him his refuge and rely on Him for his strength and wisdom. Life offers the unexpected; some are pleasant and some are not but when our focus is on **Him** the unpleasant ones seem more bearable and the surprises come as a bonus.

We end up learning and growing either ways. Acceptance and a staunch belief is key to keeping our sanity in an ever-changing, transient world. Change is never easy, especially when we get used to our comfort zones. The change was to come and it would turn my world upside down! Was I ready? Is anyone ever ready?

Do not be anxious about anything, but in every situation, by prayer and petition, with thanksgiving, present your requests to God. And the peace of God, which transcends all understanding, will guard your hearts and your minds in Christ Jesus. - Philippians 4:6-7

Chapter 13

The Embrace Of Grace

It was the morning of the 13th of August 1988 when Rony awakened me from a deep sleep at 3:00 am in the morning. "Milly! Milly!" he gently patted my arm. I jumped up like there was an earthquake! "What Happened!" I shouted, knowing instinctively that something was wrong! "Don't shout! Or you'll wake the children!" He said whispering. "I don't feel very well and I think we should go to the hospital, just to be on the safe side."

I immediately began to pack a few things and we let the children sleep on so as to not cause alarm. We left quietly as there were a few hours before they would awaken.

We arrived at the Holy Family hospital in the wee hours of the morning. It was quiet and at the emergency section, Rony told the nurse in charge at the time, that he believed he had suffered a heart attack and wanted to be admitted to the ICU immediately to be monitored. She was taken aback at his candour. If it were indeed a heart attack would he be able to talk or even come down on his own like that? She didn't seem to get the urgency of the situation. Half believing him, she tried to calm him down and stall till she could get the heart specialist in to take a look at him. "I cannot wait for the Heart Surgeon to get here to tell me something I already know!" He said firmly.

I had begun to panic inside as that was the first time he had said that out loud since he woke me. I contained my anxiety and began to pray that she listened to him and he was given the attention he needed. "I can admit you to the normal ward, sir! Once the doctor has examined you, we can move you to the ICU if required, later."

Rony almost barked back, losing his patience. "I'm paying for the ICU and I would like to be admitted to one right away!" She went inside for a moment to speak with her seniors and came back a minute later asking for a wheelchair to take Rony to the Intensive Care Unit. We made eye contact and he gave me an assuring look as if to say he knew exactly what he was doing. I tagged along by his side and as they hooked him up to the ventilator, took an Electro-Cardio-Gram test and they began taking his blood pressure, I just kept lifting him up in prayer.

I felt helpless and knew that in these times of utter confusion, instead of being overwhelmed it was much wiser to leave the situation in the hands of God. He knew what was to come and he was in control, I assured myself. I did my part to reassure Rony as well. To make sure he stayed calm. He didn't say much as if he wanted to preserve the little energy he had left. It was obvious he had gone through something and he knew that feeling well as it had happened before. Besides he had read up so many books on what to expect when you're having a heart attack, so I had to believe he had felt one coming on or he wouldn't have been so determined to get to the ICU.

I trusted and prayed. I kept having to intercede over and over and the positive prayers and my vibe of quiet support was indeed a huge relief for Rony. The last thing he needed was to have me go hysterical on him. The heart specialist Dr. Apte was summoned and he came over at around 3:45 am or so. He looked at the ECG and the reports. He looked up at Rony's calm face and said. "You've suffered a minor Myocardial Infarction. Thank God you had the wisdom to get yourself admitted. Your heartbeat and nervous system seem stable now. Let's keep you under close observation."

They discussed what had happened and I heard Rony speak about what he had felt for the first time and I have to admit it wasn't easy to hear. He explained how it had begun in the night while he was asleep. He suddenly awoke in a cold sweat. He felt short of breath and felt as if his head was bursting. He felt a sudden pain in his chest that went away as fast as it had come and recurred every now and then. He had immediately taken his prescribed tablets to lower cholesterol build up and a coagulant to thin the blood and prevent high blood pressure.

He had felt weak like his whole world was coming to an end and the dizziness made him scared to attempt to get up from the bed. At one stage, he felt like a truck had run over his chest. The tightness and indigestion were unmistakable. He realised he was having a heart attack and he knew that he couldn't waste any more time getting himself admitted so he could be administered the right drugs and be monitored by professionals. He had done all he could under the circumstances. The doctor was very impressed with his level of knowledge, his due-diligence and proactive actions. "You might just have saved your own life, Mr. Pereira! Now if all patients were like you we wouldn't have so many casualties! Well done!"

Rony wasn't in the clear quite yet. He would need absolute bed rest, the right diet and nutrition and constant medication for him to recuperate. They would have to keep monitoring his progress. The reports clearly indicated that there was a scar on his heart tissue. It would need time to heal. I prayed that the good Lord, who had healed him completely before would work his wonders again.

I called up Josephine and Eric to join me in the hospital so I could go back home to send the kids to school. I didn't want to let up that there was something wrong with their dad, lest they worry. It was best that they were in school so I could concentrate on Rony.

Josephine arrived a little later and just held my hand. Tears welled up as they always did when I felt someone's empathy and concern. I held the floodgates in check. There wasn't time to have any meltdown. I rushed off to get the kids ready. I quickly picked up some breakfast along the way from 'Hersh' bakery which luckily opened early morning. They asked where dad had gone and I told them he was admitted to hospital but downplayed the seriousness of it all. "He just needs to be monitored. You know daddy, right! He doesn't like to take any chances." I assured them he was fine and that they could see him soon.

The kids were very worried and concerned despite my attempts to soft peddle it. They were so supportive and began quoting my own words to them. "Don't worry mum! Just leave him in God's hands and everything will be alright." I needed those soothing voices of affirmation and those sweet hands of comfort on my shoulder. I hugged them goodbye and rushed back to the hospital to relieve Josephine who had her own children to take care of. I thanked God for her unrelenting support. It's true she was like a sister I never had.

The days that followed were spent mostly in the hospital and home. I remember attending early 6:00 am mass in the beautiful chapel in the hospital itself. I recall a priest and a nun going on their rounds and before they could pass the I.C.U, I quickly requested if the priest could take communion to Rony too and he obliged. Rony received Holy Communion and the priest blessed him. I was so appreciative. I'd spend the night at the hospital and my mum moved in so the children weren't alone. I'd head back home to make sure the children could be attended to and I could see them off so their lives were not disrupted and they could cope better with their dad's hospitalisation.

I remember the morning when I was sitting by Rony's side. He was very quiet and reflective. I thought he might be worrying about the situation so to ease his mind I offered to pass him his favourite sports magazines. He could spend hours reading about world politics, sports and listen to the BBC news on the radio.

That morning, instead of taking the magazines from me willingly, he just passed it up and placed his hand on the book on his chest – the Bible. "Milly where is your faith? I have Him with me now. That's all I need!" I realised he had been reading the word of God from the Bible and had paused to reflect on a passage that had touched him.

I felt so overjoyed and reassured that it was futile to worry about him being worried.

He spoke to me about what was on his mind with a caveat that I remain silent and just absorb what he wanted to spill out. It was important that he was able to 'hand over' his plans for the future, just in case. I held myself together and promised him that I would not interrupt him. He told me to sell the Bandra home and move to Goa. He said, with the money, I should educate the children, and send Albert to a management school abroad and not to compromise on their education in any way. He told me of his financial situation, to write to the shipping company he was with and inform them of his hospitalisation. He just emptied his 'To Do' list to me and thanked me for not getting emotional or for not stopping him for once.

The doctor arrived for his usual check up and read the reports. He thought to discuss with Rony the possibility of a bypass surgery. His recommendation was to have Rony moved to Hinduja Hospital where he was also consulting at, as he felt the hospital was better equipped to handle a critical operation.

He said, "Your heart is weak, Mr. Pereira! The scars are not going to heal as well as they did the last time this happened. You were much younger then so the body was able to recuperate but now you're older and the heart has been weakened significantly. You're always open to the risk of blockages occurring again and why risk that going forward. The bypass has increasingly become a new lease on life. If all goes well, it has the potential to restore your health and that is invaluable to you given your young family."

Rony listened with interest and he seemed to agree. I had begun to get nervous. A bypass operation was serious. Though the Doctor was skilled, it was always a risk. I immediately began to pray. "Lord, if this is your will then help me to surrender Rony in your hands." The nervousness diminished but by no means vanished.

The doctor explained in great detail what the operation would entail. In this operation, a surgeon uses a vessel from another part of the body to create a detour around a blocked artery thus restoring blood flow to the heart. Rony was of course, sceptical of whether or not he was the right candidate for bypass and what were the risks involved. The doctor reassured him that he was as he had gone through repeated heart attacks and blockages in his arteries and the severity and weakness in his left ventricle made it necessary to do this operation to extend his life. The pros of a bypass surgery were that it successfully removed blockages and they had the potential to reoccur only after 10 to 15 years at the least. But he explained that Bypass was not a cure and if Rony wasn't careful with his diet, exercise regime and a healthy lifestyle, his bypass could result in the same fate with new clogs in the arteries.

Rony realised that is was a good option. He trusted the doctor's ability and recommendation. He discussed with the doctor in great depth; the pros, the cons, the side effects, the post-operative care and the cost. After much deliberation, he decided to go ahead with the operation. It was probably the biggest decision he had ever taken in his entire life.

I continued to pray. I only knew how to surrender my mixed feelings and reservations to him. I believed that if this were right for Rony, then God would allow it to happen. He would oversee the whole operation and guide the hands of the doctors. I interceded every moment from then on. "Praise you, Jesus!" Thank you, Jesus!" is all I could keep repeating over and over as if, if I stopped praying the words, it would somehow mean I had stopped believing that God knew what he was permitting to happen.

The hospital staff were instructed to make the necessary arrangements to have Rony moved to Hinduja that very day in the afternoon. It would have to be under Intensive Care supervision at all times. Albert, didn't go to college that morning and joined me in the hospital, so he could accompany us to Hinduja. I had told him about the tentative plan but had kept it from the girls who were in school at the time. Noella was in her 10th grade, an important year for her so I didn't want her to miss classes and my youngest, Roslynn was too young to upset her so.

Ralph, Doreen's husband joined me in the hospital that morning too as I had informed them about the plans to shift Rony that day.

Rony had just been briefed on the benefits of an open-heart bypass surgery and had poured out all his worries to me – But the what ifs, the hypotheticals were causing him stress. Suddenly his pulse rate went up and the monitors began to show erratic waves. There were beeps and sounds and I began to panic inside just as much as the machine, which seemed to be going haywire. I charged out to call the nurse immediately but they had already begun rushing in. I wasn't sure what was happening...I was asked to wait outside the I.C.U as they attended to the patient. I remember there was a wheelchair just outside and I sat in it waiting. Suddenly, there was an alarm bell sounded from within and nurses came running out signalling wildly. Doctors rushed in with equipment to administer artificial resuscitation. All the while, we held each other's hands and continued to pray that Rony was going to pull through, not knowing or being able to comprehend the seconds that followed; they all seemed like an eternity. Everything within me, in those couple of seconds, yelled in utter alarm and desperation. I wanted to run to him, to hold him in my arms, to drive everyone out and just hold on to him – to never let him go!

Part of me wanted to scream. "What's happening Lord? Why!? Do you love me, Lord? Then Why? Why? Why?!!" I knew I had Albert with me and I had to be strong for him, for myself, for Rony. I was asked a question back in that dark moment; a question that instantly brought me back from the helpless insanity I felt overcoming me, "You said you trusted me! Can you surrender?" At that moment, I felt a surreal peace envelope my entire being as if God himself was caressing me, stroking my head like a little child and assuring me that everything would be alright. I felt lifted from darkness into light!

My whole life I lay at His feet. I surrendered completely to His will! "You are my Lord and my God! You know what is best for me, my children and most importantly for Rony! I surrender him into your hands!" The minute I uttered and felt every word of this silent prayer, I was engulfed with a sense of peace, grace and tranquillity I had never ever experienced before. Just a moment before I had felt desperate and overwhelmed with anxiety and suddenly I was feeling a surreal strength from within.

God's Grace alone helped me survive the news that came forth from the I.C.U that day! I had walked towards the I.C.U and when I saw the doctor, I just knew. I said, "He's gone!?" "Yes! He said. He had been wondering how to break the news and I made it easier for him. "We tried our best Mrs. Pereira! He didn't make it I'm afraid!" The forlorn faces of the emerging doctors and nurses was the worst possible sight I have ever had to see in my lifetime; the impending feeling of hopelessness that their faces and expressions were resigned to! "I'm sure you did! Thank you Doctor!" I replied calmly.

Albert let out a yelp of despair! "Aaaaaaah! Dad!!!Dad!" He ran forward to enter the I.C.U and was held back by the nurses. He shouted the loudest I have ever heard this quiet and reserved child shout! He yelled, stamped and denied. I held him as tight as I could and I remember just calming him down. "Jesus has taken daddy! Albert! He is with Jesus now! He is not suffering anymore! He is happy! I know he is!"

"I WANT TO SEE DAD!" he yelled. "I want to hug him." I wanted to too! But the hospital regulations wouldn't permit it. I hugged Albert close and tight. I was dealing with my own grief and his and I felt the pain gnawing at my heart and thought of the girls and how I'd have to break it to them gently. How does a mother tell their child that they will never ever see their father again. The finality of that broke my heart and would most definitely break theirs too.

"Yet sorrowful but always rejoicing!" were words from the Bible that came to my mind like God was talking to me. It was the only way I could explain the serenity I felt. I had feared death all my life. It was a phobia I had to deal with. I feared the death of my loved ones more than my own and I often found myself praying that I would not outlive my parents or my husband or my children. Every single day I prayed for their protection and long life. The unthinkable had happened.

We were left alone to fend for ourselves in the BIG BAD world! Was I adult enough to hold it together? Was my faith strong enough to rely on God, now, more than ever? Did I have it in me to pull through widowhood? I was a WIDOW!

I looked at Albert and was simply swept away with an overwhelming feeling that he and his sisters were not orphans and I would do everything in my power to make sure I was a rock solid mum to them. I wanted to make it alright. I wanted to say to them, "Everything will be OK!" I knew I had to be strong and I cried out internally for God's help. I cried out to Rony too! "I know you're here watching helplessly as we weep! Pray for me, Ron! Pray that I may bear this pain and that we may survive!"

They had covered his head with a white sheet when they brought his body out to be taken to the morgue. They handed me a form to fill and said that the doctor would prepare the post mortem report. After the post-mortem was performed and verified, they would be able to give me a death certificate with which I could claim the body from the morgue for the funeral. I felt numb. I heard the words being uttered but was too shocked to take it all in.

I had called Eric and Josephine and cried on the phone when I blurted the news to them. They were distraught and we all wept. They hurried over to the hospital and handled all the details; the formalities I didn't have any inclination to take care of at the time, understandably. I wanted to soothe Albert's shock. To take away the emptiness we both felt. I prayed with him that morning. We prayed a prayer of surrender, of forgiveness and for peace for Rony's departed soul. I felt him. I knew he was around. I knew his feeling of helplessness, confusion and equal shock. I wanted to release him of our baggage. Perhaps the weight of our attachment to him, the feeling of guilt that he had abandoned us or the feeling of remorse and any negativity our own fear and loss might have been binding him with.

The prayer filled me with a grace that could only come from above. It's as if my tears had all fallen and dried up! I felt a renewed strength and a purpose to be strong for the children was driving my resolve to hold it together.

Albert became very quiet and sullen. He was holding in the feeling of outrage. He couldn't bring himself to accept the fact that his dad was gone! – Had been snatched away like that so early! The feeling of helplessness was too much for such a young one to endure! We both went home and I called the girls' school to inform them and to request that the girls be sent home early that day. I also requested that they keep the news from them, as I wanted to be the one to break it to them as gently as I possibly could; The eternity of it was just too overwhelming! They were so young! Vulnerable darlings! I dreaded the moment. To see their faces grimace with the pain of loss! The heart is so fragile, so tender and the face a live reflection of that emotion!

Reliving the anguish over and over again, with them and with each of his dear ones I would have to eventually inform, was heart wrenching.

Noella had been sullen that whole morning so much so that the teachers kept asking her what was wrong. She just began to cry profusely, the tears rolling down uncontrollably but with no sound leaving her mouth. She always cried silently like that.

They had summoned the class teacher and thought that perhaps she was feeling ill. She assured them that nothing was wrong with her health and that she was only worried about her dad, who was in the hospital. So when the teachers received the news of her dad's passing they were very sorry and told Noella that it was best that she went home early that day. All the way back home, she had cried and Roslynn, who was only in class 5 then, kept asking her if she had got a bad score in her test papers or she had been scolded by any teacher but she just kept silent all the way with tears rolling down her cheeks.

When they arrived home, the next-door neighbours had kept their door open with the idea to intervene so they could have something to eat before finding out the news. They were outside the door and quickly whisked them away to give them lunch at their home. Noella refused to eat and she demanded to go home first. "Where's mum? I want to go home!" she said firmly, almost rudely! Her intuition was demanding answers.

I heard the raised voices and opened the door. I saw her swollen face and I thought she already knew. "Jesus has taken daddy, baby! He's gone to heaven!" I blurted out, now crying myself. I couldn't hold the tears back any longer. They came pouring out like a river downstream. She cried aloud for the first time! "No! Daddy!!! I want to see daddy!!" she cried bitterly, hugging me tightly. Roslynn had been distracted by the good food and heard her sister crying so loudly that she left what she was eating and came running out. She saw us both hugging each other and knew that something was not right. "What's wrong, Mummy?!" she asked almost hesitatingly…I took her in my arms and told her that her father was in heaven and that he was happy there as he didn't have to be in the hospital or suffer anymore.

She patted me as if to console me and I still remember what she said, "Don't worry mummy! Just pretend he's gone on the ship, then you won't cry!" I couldn't believe how her nine-year-old mind was able to come up with this ingenious self-preservation technique so instantly! She was a positive thinker just like her dad! "I'll do that my pet! It's a very good idea!" I said and hugged her so she could take her time to absorb and understand what had really happened.

Many years later she told me of an apparition she had seen as a kid during assembly that ill-fated day. She said to me, "I had a day vision mum! Dad came to say bye to me during assembly. He appeared and I said, "Hi!" Because he was at the door and then I gestured if I could go out and he shook his head and made a sign as if to reassure me that everything was going be fine and that he'll be watching. Then he said, "bye!" and vanished. I wanted to run out of assembly hall to see if he was still around but couldn't. He was smiling and I got a chance to say goodbye. It happened when I was wide awake."

The funeral was fixed so that Rony's brothers could fly down from Kuwait and the U.K. It would take them time so we deferred the funeral to 18th of August. We made arrangements to write an obituary in the newspapers and to inform everyone we knew; relatives and friends. Eric and Josephine and our dear friends Doreen and Ralph helped so much! They were just there in our time of need, holding the fort and doing the hard work.

Noella's Pencil Sketch of her dad – A creative expression of her grief.

The children wanted to be left alone. Albert wished he could shy away from everyone and not have to face the many curious questions, the forlorn shrugging shoulders and shaking heads of distant relatives he had never seen before in his life! On the day of the funeral he began to shout loudly in the bedroom, "Why can't they all leave? Why do they all have to be here?" I had to calm him down but could understand how he felt. It's difficult as it is, then to have to deal with socialising and putting up a brave front when all you want is peace and moments of quiet reflection. He had a melt down when one relative demanded to know why they weren't informed sooner and another wanted to know every detail of how it happened and why it happened.

Those moments were tough to deal with and the loss of a beloved one gnaws at your heart like a rat chewing slowly. The pain was numbing, gripping, choking because of the constant lump you felt in your throat and blinding because of the tears that would well up without warning.

I saw Noella take her father's towel, the one he had used last and she put it to her face and just buried herself in it inhaling his scent, holding on to the last shred of what was left of him on earth. She was a sensitive child and was always in her own little world, dreaming, imagining and thinking. The loss of her dad, who she adored, was a huge blow for her and she coped in her own withdrawn sort of way. Holding dear all his possessions, preserving his towel and his shirts. She went through all the old photographs so she could feel close to him and would cry silently as she relived vivid memories.

On the day he passed away, she found it in herself to express her grief in such a unique way! She quietly took one of her favourite photos of him, the one taken on the bridge with his hair blowing in the wind, which he had sent to me in the mail. It read, "Finally the camera has been kind." It was a stunning and natural shot and he had this very, whimsical smile on his face as he looked far out into the ocean.

His windswept hair added to the charm of his mystical expression. Noella gently propped the photograph up on the table and began sketching his face with a drawing pencil. Three to four hours later, she was done and the sketch was simply marvellous! She was in her teens but the drawing was one of a professional artist. She had captured Rony so beautifully with such accurate proportion and shading; every nuance, every wisp, every glint and every fine line of this fine man; a tribute in art form. How wonderfully creative and what an outpouring of her emotion it was! We all cried as we admired the sketch.

He was with us in spirit and we felt him smile through. I had to print the obituary the very next day and was thinking of appropriate words for the bookmark. It suddenly came to me in a flash! Normally it was Rony with the talent for writing poetry or flowery language. So I was happy that I was inspired by one of his favourite songs by Frank Sinatra, 'My Way'. I was thinking of Rony and all that he embodied when he was alive. I wanted a fitting tribute but it also had to be concise. I put pen to paper and began choosing the verse. I realised just how appropriate the whole song was! I had to make it brief so I just took a small verse from it that was true to Rony's life. I placed the order for the mortuary cards but they arrived with Rony's face all dark, in shadows and not very visible. We took copies of Rony's picture and actually had to glue it on each bookmark ourselves to salvage the situation. I was stressed out but it turned out to be so appropriate and the coloured photos were so much better in the end.

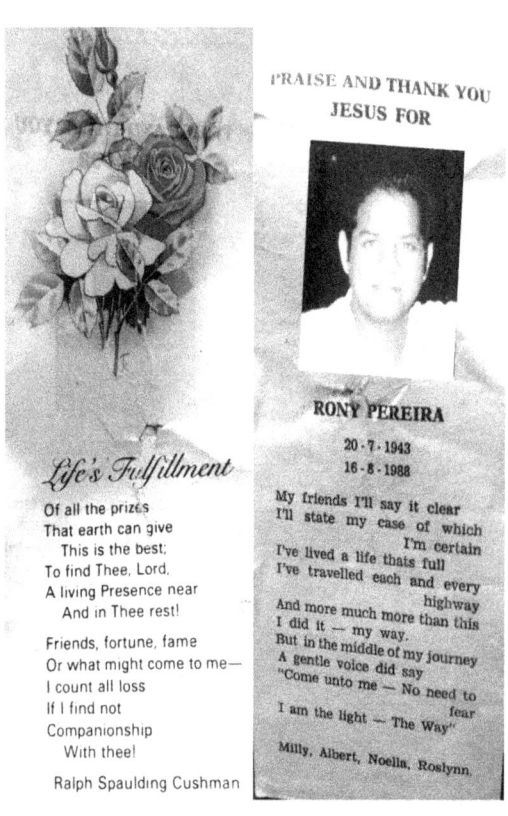

The obituary with lyrics from 'My Way' - a song Rony loved to sing and was so true to his own life.

The funeral service was held at our parish in St. Andrews Church nearby. It was at 4:00 pm, followed by the burial at the cemetery in Mahalaxmi, where Rony's ancestors were buried. He was sentimental and would have wanted it that way.

His brothers were both grief-stricken when they heard the news and immediately flew down from Kuwait and the U.K. Rony had such a loving relationship with all his siblings. They were 5 of them including two younger sisters. The youngest was living close by at the time, so she was there for the funeral but his other sister could not make it down at such short notice; she lives in America. She spoke to me on the phone and sent me a beautiful letter with comforting words and reflections from verses she had painstakingly hand written.

I saw Rony's lifeless body after he had been brought to the church, we didn't bring his body home although we were told it was a tradition, as I didn't want the children to have that negative imagery associated with him, in the home. I think it was a wise choice. Rony looked peaceful. There was a calm serenity on his face like as if he had suffered no pain. But his body was cold and it was such a shock to touch his fingers and feel as if they were hard blocks of stone almost. His soul had left and the lifelessness in a body that was once my husband, left me feeling a void I wasn't certain, would ever be filled!

The church was packed to capacity and we all sat on the front seat. We wore solemn colours. I don't understand what came over me, but I suddenly felt the urge to say a prayer of thanksgiving for Rony at the mass. I went to the pulpit and simply let my heart out! No tear dropped, no stutter, no hesitation. The Holy Spirit had taken over my tongue.

I thanked God for the gift of Rony to the family for 18 years and for the legacy he had left behind; the bank of cherished memories he had created with his zest for life, his sense of humour, his magnanimity and his generosity of heart. I had learnt to live enthusiastically because of him. He had accepted me with my failings, faults and loved me unconditionally. He was a loving father to my children and was a living example of God's compassion. I knew then, why they used to say, 'God takes His most beloved early.'

The words just flew out of me like they weren't even my own! I had always been so reluctant to speak in public and taking the microphone was out of the question! I was as stunned at my forwardness, strength and surreal calm as others were that day. They all came up to me to say how touched they were with my impromptu prayer. I had accepted his passing with a God-given grace. I relied on God's love and he was my spouse thereafter.

Noella had agreed to sing one of her favourite hymns for the funeral service at the graveyard. She had inherited Rony's talent for singing and had a rich, deep voice, much more mature sounding for her age. She sang, "You gave a song" by Evie Tornquist Karlsson. The lyrics were from a psalm from the bible, which I'd like to share....

You lifted me out of a pit
You set my feet upon a solid rock
Put a new song in my mouth
Gave me reason to sing
You gave me a song of praise
Chorus: You gave a song
Made me go on
Singing praises to your name

You are my Lord!

You're my God!
You're forever more the same
I want to praise you!
Praise you! Praise You! Praise You!
Praise your Holy name
You gave a song!
Made me go on, praising your name!

Now every day, has true meaning!
I know the reason why you placed me here!
I've devoted my life
To bring honour to you!
You gave me a song of praise!

She sang her heart out and cried in between but continued to sing and it was so touching to see her connect with her dad. The words were so appropriate and comforted our aching hearts.

Perhaps the most difficult part of a funeral service is the parting with the body you've loved for so long. To actually see him for the last time, to allow the coffin to be shut over his face, to let go, to see him being lowered in front of our eyes, to throw sand over the coffin, to remind ourselves that dust he was and to dust he will return; it was the final moment of truth, a truth we were desperately trying to forget, to cope with and to deny. We were being denied *HIM* and that hurt!!

The two days after his passing were like a whirlwind of activity with relatives flying in, things to be done, processes to be followed, paperwork to be taken care of, arrangements to be made, people to be informed, ads to be put out, money to be withdrawn etc. etc. It all happened so fast. We didn't have time to breathe or take a moment to ourselves.

I needed time to reflect, time to calm my own nerves. I found comfort in the 'Streams in the desert' by L.B Cowman, a soulful daily devotional readings and reflections Christian book, which had verses from the bible and a contemporary perspective on each verse for the calendar day. Very often I found God spoke to me through this book. It had become Rony's favourite book towards the end too and he would get just the wisdom he needed for that moment.

He used to like one particular reading very much as he related to it so much. Very often during his illness, when he was confined to the four walls of the home recuperating, he'd get claustrophobic as he was an outdoorsy person by nature so it was difficult for him to stay put. He'd open this reading he had found and would keep reading it over and over again. He had even book-marked it so he could find it easily. I took the book again and when I opened the page to the bookmark he had placed, my whole body shook to see which page it was. It was the 16th of August!!!

It had a reference to the line "I waited patiently for the Lord. Psalm 40:1. I took the bible to read which one it was and I was pleasantly surprised to read the whole Psalm – *"In Waiting, I Waited for the Lord! - I waited patiently for the Lord; and he inclined unto me, and heard my cry. He brought me up also out of a horrible pit, out of the miry clay and set my feet upon a rock, and established my goings. And he hath put a new song in my mouth, even praise unto our God: many shall see it, and fear, and shall trust in the Lord."*

The reading he had loved to read had a contemplative message that waiting was far more difficult as waiting required patience and patience remains a rare virtue. But it reassures that God has a purpose in all of His delays and that once we learn to wait for the Lord's leading in everything, we will know the strength that comes with even steadiness. Waiting; keeping ourselves faithful to *His* leading; this is the secret of strength!

It questioned whether life could be considered a failure for someone compelled to stand still and forced into inaction and required to watch the tides of life from ashore. So apt for Rony I thought as I read through it. It reiterated that victory was to be won by standing still and quietly waiting. Yet this is extremely hard to do. It requires much more courage to stand and wait and still not lose heart or hope but to submit to the will of God and give up opportunities for work, leaving the honours to others. It encouraged us to be quiet, yet confident and continue to rejoice while others go about their busy lives.

Rony had been compelled to wait, be still and find himself and God in the stillness in the months that led up to his passing. I felt so glad to know he had sought out God, kept reading the Lord's word and his hands were so often on the Bible.

I felt the Lord speak directly to me. I felt His assurance and His outstretched arms and tender loving and soothing voice as if He knew I was just a baby and I needed to be lifted and carried and cajoled. It was also the ***exact same*** Psalm from the song Noella had sung at the funeral service. She was destined to sing it that day! There are no coincidences.

I kept reading 'Streams in the Desert' as it was like my translator or walkie-talkie with God and such a connection with Rony! In hindsight, I was so captivated by the messages I was receiving that I didn't allow myself to be pulled into fruitless 'what ifs' or 'if only. I was sitting in church only 3 days after Rony's passing and these negative thoughts began to pervade my mind. I wondered if I had done everything I could. What if I had been stronger, smarter, a better planner and insisted that we go the U.K to attend to Rony's medical needs at the right time, perhaps he would still be alive. I was admonishing myself for being too dumb, too meek and not having the presence of mind. I picked up the laminated folder in front of me to fan myself – It had responsorial psalms for the entire week. My eyes fell upon one and It read, 1 Samuel 2:6, *"The LORD brings death and makes alive; he brings down to the grave and raises up."* I was reminded that He was the almighty authority over life and death and that nothing I could have done or not done would have made any difference whatsoever. I could have taken Rony to the ends of the earth and made sure he received the best medical attention available, spent all the money we had but it would not change the inevitable. Rony's death was predestined.

These negative thoughts can so easily pull us into feelings of regret and keep us trapped in our misery. The secret to healing the hurt and the void is closure, which most of us yearn for – It's true of all experiences we treasure that don't work out the way we want it to. God provided the closure I needed.

I read the next day's passage and it was as if it was written exclusively for me, as it was all about a Captain, his story of his passenger George Mueller's unrelenting faith and how he reaches the shore for an important meeting after encountering stormy seas and the thickest of fog. He had said a simple prayer and was convinced that the storm would clear.

" "Captain, I have known my Lord for fifty-seven years, and there has never been even a single day that I have failed to get an audience with the King. Get up, Captain, and open the door, and you will see that the fog is gone." "I got up, and indeed the fog was gone. And on Saturday afternoon George Mueller was in Quebec for his meeting. If our love were just simpler, we would take Him at His word; and our lives would be all sunshine, in the sweetness of our Lord." "

I said a silent prayer to the Lord to renew me with this very simplistic faith. I needed to cling on to him, as I had never done before! I was excited with this word. I knew and fully grasped now why it was called – "The Good news of the Lord!" I flipped those golden pages to August 18th, the day of the funeral – It had a beautiful poem, which had lines that touched me,

> ....*One long, dark moment,*
> *And no friend I saw, save Jesus only.*
> *But oh! so tenderly*
> *He led me on*
> *And up, and spoke to me such words of cheer,*
> *Such secret whisperings of*
> *His wondrous love,*
> *That soon I told Him all my grief and fear,*
> *And leaned on His strong arm confidingly.*
> *And then I found my footsteps quickened,*
> *And light unspeakable, the rugged way*
> *Illumined, such light as only can be seen*
> *In close companionship with God.*
> *A little while, and we will meet again*
> *The loved and lost;*
>
> *And tender recollections rushing back*
> *Of life now passed,*
> *I think one memory*
> *More dear and sacred than the rest will rise,*
> *And we who gather in the golden streets,*
> *Will oft be stirred to speak with grateful love*
> *Of that dark day Jesus called us to climb*
> *Some narrow steep, leaning on Him alone.*
> *There is never a majestic mountain*
> *without a deep valley,*
> *and there is no birth without pain."*
> *Daniel Crawford*

It was like Rony had written this poem himself. He was saying to me, that God had called him and that he was not alone and I wasn't either. It was like he was reassuring me that we would indeed meet again. These words of assurance brought tears of gratitude to my eyes.

> One night I dreamed I was walking along the beach with the Lord. Scenes from my life flashed across the sky. In each, I noticed footprints in the sand. Sometimes there were two sets of footprints; other times there was only one.
>
> During the lowest times of my life I could see only one set of footprints, so I said, "Lord, you promised me, that you would walk with me always. Why, when I have needed you most, would you leave me?"
>
> The Lord replied, "My precious child, I love you and would never leave you. The times when you have seen only one set of footprints, it was then that I carried you."

I knew that I wasn't alone! God was always walking with me and it reminded me of the beautiful 'Footprints' poem – The times when I didn't see two pairs of footprints in the sand, and I thought he had forgotten me or left me alone, were the times he was actually carrying me through it all. This was that time! I felt His firm and loving hands cradling me through the toughest time in my entire life!

Every day he built me up in my strength and in my resolve to place my trust in him. That is all he wanted from me to say "Yes!" to His will in simplistic faith, just like Mother Mary had done 2000 years before. I recalled a poem Noella had recited at school, which I had chosen for her from 'Streams in the Desert' for her elocution competition. A few excerpts are worth sharing as I re-read the lines, they built me up even more. …

> "Self-pity said to me:
> "You poor, poor thing, you have too much To do.
> Your life is far too hard.
> This heavy load will crush you soon."

"Ah yes, it will break and crush my life; I cannot bear this constant strain
Of endless, aggravating cares; they are too great for such as I."
So thus my heart consoled itself,
'Enjoying misery',
When lo! A 'still small voice' distinctly said,
"'Twas sent to lift you, not to crush."

I saw at once my great mistake.
My place was not beneath the load but on the top!
God meant it not that I should carry it.
He sent it here to carry me.

To lie and cringe beneath
One's load means death, but life and power
Await all those who dare to rise above.
Our burdens are our wings; on them
We soar to higher realms of grace;

O paradox of Heaven.
The load
We think will crush was sent to lift us Up to God!
Then, soul of mine, Climb up!

Within His word is found
The key, which opens His secret stairs;
Alone with Christ, secluded there,
We mount our loads and rest in Him."
- Mary Butterfield

She had recited it with so much feeling and maturity but it was too heavy and deep for her school level and the judges made a special mention of her piece sighting it as an example. They felt that students should choose age-appropriate pieces. I guess they were right. It was a bit to high-flown perhaps with religious connotations that they weren't comfortable with, in a multi-cultural school. But though Noella was so young, she had grasped the essence of the emotion, the lesson along with the paradox and had delivered it with the maturity of an adult and I was proud of her! Her piece stood out for its emotion and message.

As I read the lines again, I understood it all over again and each line began to have new meaning and relevance to my circumstance. Earlier

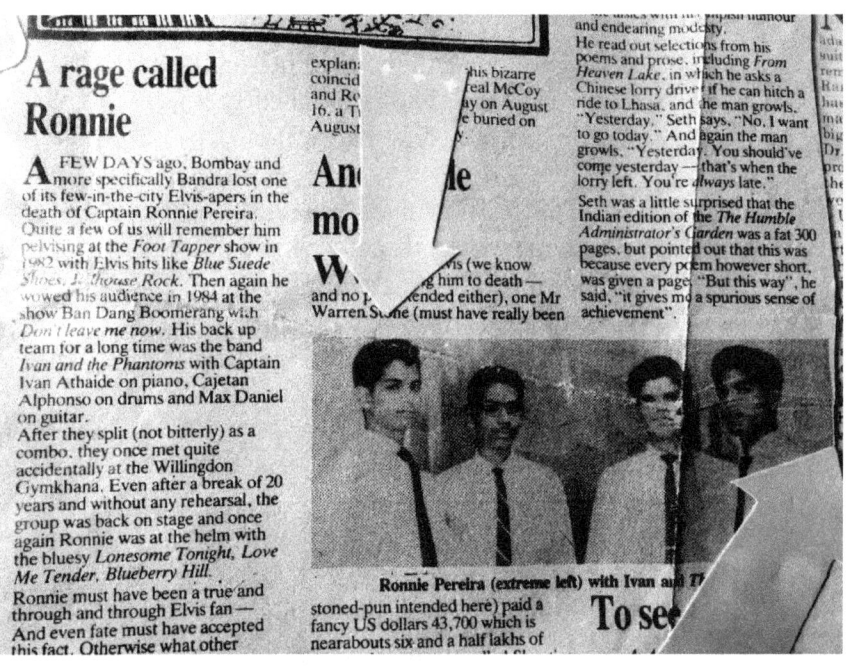

A newspaper article that appeared in the Mid-Day after Rony's funeral in August 1988.

I had liked the piece for its poetic passion but reading it afresh, allowed me to truly 'get it.'

I recall the day of the funeral; one of Rony's friends came up to me and mentioned that Rony was such a huge Elvis Presley fan and it so happened that it was the exact same day, 11 years prior, that the King of rock-n-roll himself had left for his heavenly abode: A Tuesday, 16th

of August 1977 & 1988 respectively. They were also buried on the same day; A Thursday, August 18th 1977 and August 18th 1988. It was such a coincidence but a fitting one.

What a marvellous sense of humour God has! He makes sure that these 'coincidences' happen to affirm His hand in every moment from the time we take our first breath to our very last. He knew how much Rony loved Elvis, and He also knew Rony always saw the funny side of things, so he made sure their departures matched to the day.

'Streams in the Desert' continued to uplift, to renew my soul, to give me constant strength. No let me rephrase that. God renewed me, uplifted me and strengthened me through this soul-stirring book! I ran to it every morning for fodder. It was a way to feel Rony's presence, to communicate with him too somehow. It made me feel closer to him in spirit and I could sense his soul connection when I reflected on the lines and read the verses from the Bible that were referred to.

It was as if he was right there beside me, smiling at me as I read and with each line acting as a balm, I felt the baggage of his guilt for having left us alone, grow lighter. I felt that with every sigh of relief I felt on my aching heart, with every release I attempted, with every surrender and with every step in faith I took, Rony was released too! Sometimes, our sorrow and our own selfish needs hold them back, the departed souls and our acceptance and reliance on God to take us through the sorrow helps them get the release their soul yearns for! With each line, I was saying to him, "Go! Rony! Go forth to your heavenly abode in peace. Rest easy! Your earthly wife is in the best hands; the hands of the Lord Jesus! There is nothing more you can and need to do!"

On August 19th, just three days after his passing, I wondered how I was so calm! Why was I smiling again? How was it possible that someone who had always been so fearful of death, was now feeling so confident? I began to question my feelings. Had my love diminished so fast?! Was I not missing Rony?! Was my heart not aching to see his face, to feel his warm hands embrace me and to feel his tender caress and kiss on my forehead? Was I not sorrowful, as I should be?

I opened the page to 'August 19th' and there was my answer! - *Sorrowful, yet always rejoicing. (2 Corinthians 6:10)* – It had an appropriate passage that followed this Psalm, with a deep explanation that hit straight home!

It explained that sorrow was beautiful, but its beauty was subtle and low key; the kind of beauty you would witness if you appreciated nature in the night, moonlight shining through in the thick of the deep woods. The passage compared sorrow's beauty to the sweet low-pitched song of a nightingale. It personified Sorrow declaring 'he' could empathize and weep in tender sympathy with those who wept but wasn't able to relate at all to those who rejoiced because joy was absolutely unknown to 'him'.

It described Joy as a beautiful woman and compared her beauty to the radiant summer morning with the happy laughter of childhood. The passage described how Joy's hair glistened with the kiss of sunshine and her voice soared upward like a skylarks. Its poetic analogies were simply ethereal comparing her steps to the march of a conqueror who has never known defeat. Joy could rejoice with anyone who rejoices, but couldn't possibly weep with those who wept as sorrow was unknown to her.

It related how 'Sorrow' longingly lamented about how he knew that they could never be united as one and Joy agreed wholeheartedly expressing how different in every way they were.

They both agreed to part ways when suddenly they both became aware of someone standing beside them. In spite of the dim light, they sensed a kingly presence and suddenly a great and holy awe over-whelmed them. They then sank to their knees before Him.

Sorrow proclaimed to see Him as the King of Joy as he saw the crown on his head and felt that the nail prints in His hands and feet were the scars of a great victory. Sorrow could feel all his sorrow melting away into deathless love and gladness and yearned to give himself to Him forever.

Joy disagreed though, for she saw Him as the King of Sorrow, and the crown on His head she saw as a crown of thorns, and the nail prints in His hands and feet were the scars of terrible agony. She also wished to give herself to Him forever for she felt that the sorrow with Him must be sweeter than any joy she could have ever known.

They suddenly realized that they were one in Him and they cried in gladness for no one but He could unite Joy and Sorrow. I read how Sorrow and Joy walked hand in hand following Him through storms and sunshine, through bitterly cold winters and the hearty warmth of summer becoming "sorrowful, yet always rejoicing."

"Sorrow, is the messenger of God to thee. He is God's angel, clothed in veils of night, With whom "we walk by faith" and "not by sight" - [2 Cor. 5:7 KJV]." I was so filled with God's message! In and through *HIM* alone can sorrow and joy be joined! My heart yearned to obey his

will for me! All I needed to do was trust and obey; my faith, unfaltering in His divine plan for me. Que Sera! Sera! Your destiny plays out and when you trust and have faith in the Lord, His plans for your life work out more wondrously than you can ever imagine!

The 16th of every month that year God sent repeated reminders my way that He was in the driver's seat in my life! On the 16th of September, Eric handed me an old cassette he found of Rony's voice recorded letter addressed to me. He had posted it to me when I was staying with my mum. That's how it had been lying with Eric, telling me how much he missed and loved me! Tears of joy filled my eyes to hear his velvet voice.

"I have been crucified with Christ; and it is no longer I who live, but Christ lives in me; and the life which I now live in the flesh I live by faith in the Son of God, who loved me, and delivered Himself up for me" - Galatians 2:20

Chapter 14

Dealing With The Loss of a Loved One

I have pondered sometimes, in dealing with the loss of our beloved, do we cling on to the memory of the person? That's natural to feel a deep sadness because we miss our loved one's presence in our daily lives so much, it hurts. Or is it the memory of loss? Reliving the moment can bring it back like it happened yesterday. Perhaps it is the memory of the emotion we felt at the time of loss? I do believe this last one; the shock, the trauma, the regret and the resultant hurt and pain is kept alive in our minds consciously or unconsciously and can be very gripping and immobilizing, keeping us from receiving a healing even with the passage of time. There's a difference between love and attachment; the former is selfless and pure and the latter self-serving. I sometimes felt that if I didn't continue to mourn I was forgetting my husband and I realised this wasn't true. My love for him never fades with time; it is eternal. He will always be a part of me but I could give myself permission to let go of the sadness; the two were not co-joined.

I remember how difficult it was to sleep at night. I'd lie awake tossing and turning. At the end of the day I'd miss the sight and presence of him next to me, I'd miss his embrace, his tenderness. I'd even miss the very things that used to irritate me, like his dirty socks lying here and there or his towel lying wet on the bed. I longed to see the bathroom well used with water and shaving cream all over the sink or the newspapers strewn all over the sofa. I'd yearn to be able to hear his voice again, discuss important things with him, and pour my heart and my worries out to him. I missed his laughter and his jokes and his singing with guitar in hand strumming dreamily. I think the toughest moment was awakening in the morning and feeling the ache of loss all over again; from blissful dreamland where everything was ok to dawn's dawning; realizing over again the harsh reality that I'd NEVER see him again in this lifetime.... It hurt and how!

It was Albert's 1st year of college and he was missing his dad's reassuring presence more than ever! How he had wished he could have talked to him about his educational path, which subjects to choose, about his peers, about sports and his goings on in this new phase of life. He also found it difficult being in a downtown, upmarket college where every single one of his friends owned cars or bikes of their own, had wallets stashed with cash to spend freely on whatever they wished.

He felt frustrated that at the time he needed him the most, he wasn't there. He was left to fend for himself and to cope. He returned one day feeling very dejected and disturbed, as he had to drop out of a college outing, as it was too expensive. He was so dying to go for it with his other buddies but he knew we could not afford it. He cried that day and broke down for the 1st time after the funeral. "I need dad!" He said. It would have been so different if he were here. Why did he leave us like this!"

I allowed him to vent his feelings and I never once tried to stop him from crying. I knew he needed to get it all out! I felt so bad for him. I wanted to make everything alright, to make up for their loss but you can only do so much! A dad is a dad and a mum's love can never replicate that unique bond they shared with their father.

I encouraged them to express their feelings. We spoke about the good memories, cried together watching precious footage of Rony, singing, walking on the ship, playing with them as children; footage of our holidays together as a family. I kept relating stories to them about their father, what he thought and wanted for each of them. His aspirations and dreams. I wanted to keep his memory alive and I knew it was important to the children to feel connected and self-expressed.

Al had grown closer to Rony during his illness and with their trip together in Malaysia. He yearned for a male perspective and conversation. The only way I knew how was to comfort him in my embrace. I suddenly thought I would share with him a passage from the Bible. "Let us just read the scripture for today and see what God is trying to tell us", I advised. He seemed disinterested and I could understand why.

I still persisted despite his reluctance. "It won't take time", I reassured. "We'll lift these feelings of frustration and loss to him and ask him to take over. He loves us more than any earthly father could ever love us, do you know that?! If your dad wanted to give you the world, how much more your heavenly father wants and desires for you?!" I had been ironing the clothes at that time and he was resting on the bed. Out of the blue, a book fell from the shelf. I picked it up and noticed that an old letter had slipped out and had fallen to the floor. It was addressed to him. It was dated 16th of November 1987, the previous year to the day!

"My *Dearest Shamshababums,*" I read the letter to Al, as he couldn't bring himself to read it. It was a letter full of encouragement but the lines that stood out the most as if Rony himself had willed that the letter was read at that precise moment were, *"As you get into a new phase of college life, things will be different and with this new found freedom comes great responsibility. I am depending on you to keep your head on your shoulders. Don't get side tracked with what everyone else is doing. You know better than to take to vices like I did. It ruined my health and I'm paying for my mistakes even today! An occasional drink with the friends is OK but promise me that you will never smoke. It is cancer waiting to happen! Look after your diet from a young age as cholesterol builds up even as young as you are. A healthy lifestyle will take you far – you can have everything in the world but if you lose your health you have nothing! Don't worry about anything. I am going to be here for you. If you need someone to talk to or confide in, you know where to come. I promise that the next year I will be with you every step of the way!"* We could feel his presence and that day we believed he was there in spirit. The letter although it was touching, was the reassurance Al needed that he would be watching over him, as he could never have done before. Words he would cherish for a long time to come! The letter was his way of communicating. I believe he willed it to fall into our laps.

Albert on his trip to Goa with his friends, while in college

Albert decided to maintain a low profile in college and used to never end up hanging out with his college buddies after sessions, as it would mean he would have to spend and he knew he didn't have that kind of money to show.

He had taken up commerce, just as his dad desired, as he decided it was a good stream to branch out into business management, advertising etc. It would open out opportunities for Albert and give him the option to pursue careers that were well paying. Albert was on the water-polo sports team and had begun to enjoy the freedom of college life.

He took up a part time job, with an entrepreneur, who had started 'Clowns-R-Us', an event management company for kids' entertainment. He had to wear a clown's suit and lead the games at kids events and birthday parties around the city. He got paid a decent amount of money per party along with tips from the hosts. He felt more confident about going out with friends. He had bought so many cool things on his trip to Malaysia so he dressed the part and none of his pals, really knew his actual situation at home.

One day, he came to me with a letter from the principal saying that Albert had not been attending his classes and 'bunking' off a lot. His attendance had fallen below the required minimum and that if he didn't makeup in the next term, they would have to take strict action like suspension etc. I was so surprised and naturally disappointed.

I explained to him, that not everything was about having a good time alone, while it was an important part of enjoying life, he had to realise that certain things needed to be prioritised and his education was one of them. I reminded him how much his dad had stressed about the importance of a good education for all the children, even requesting me to sell the Bandra place and use the money to make sure that all the children got into top-notch institutions. "A good education secures their future Milly! Don't ever compromise on it." He had said this over and over again. I explained that paying his tuition fees and to continue to stay in Bandra would cost us a lot of money and with dad gone, there was little to go around. I was struggling, as it is to make ends meet and the last thing I needed was for him to start acting up and causing me additional stress.

Only two weeks after Rony's passing, I was offered a job by St. Stanislaus as a substitute teacher, standing in for a teacher who had gone for a holiday to the gulf. They said that they were Ok if I chose to join up after the months mind mass, but I was ready to join immediately. I said, "If this has come my way now, I will take it up without hesitation, as I know it is meant for me.". I hadn't taught for so many years but I adjusted well. It kept me engaged and busy in the mornings, brought in some income, however meagre it was, to run the home as the coffers were being emptied every day on the fixed costs; maintenance, school fees, college fees, groceries and the list went on.

My mum moved in with us to help with the kids and with the cooking and I was so grateful for her support. Time used to fly by. I used to be so busy with the little ones in school that I would forget all about my worries and anxieties and when I came home, attending to the children and their studies etc. left me no time to pity myself or wallow in any way! By the end of the day, I was nothing but exhausted! I would get sound sleep as soon as I hit the pillow. Days turned into months and months turned into years as this routine went on... I had submitted to God's plan for me and he saw to it that I was well.

Albert was ashamed that his callous attitude was causing me anxiety and promised to begin attending his sessions regularly and he was true to his word. His grades improved and I was thankful I never got called in to see the principal again.

I did get a huge bill at the end of the term though and because I didn't have that chunk of money at hand I kept deferring it till one day, I received a note from the college threatening that if the outstanding fees were not paid on time, his seat for the next year would be opened to another deserving student. There were waiting lists for these colleges. I was given a due date and it was fast approaching. The family had been a great help during the funeral, with arrangements etc. and I didn't want to borrow money from them. I felt helpless.

I prayed to the Lord to guide me and help me out. I made up my mind to part with my ancestral bangles, gifted to me by my mother, when one morning, Doreen walks in, completely surprising me with a gesture, I will never forget. She said she had been praying to God to use her as an instrument and while meditating, suddenly, out of the blue, a thought was implanted into her mind from nowhere! "Milly needs money. Give her some." She was sure she had not thought about it earlier or had any intention prior to that moment.

She simply obeyed and came over with some hot fish curry she had so lovingly made for us and an envelope containing the exact amount of money that was needed for the term fees. She said I didn't have to return it, that they gave a certain amount of money to the needy and that she was directed to give it to me. I was astounded at how God looks after His children and how He uses His beloved too. I praised Him for His glorious ways and for keeping His promise to look after the widow and her children.

Just about a month after joining St. Stanislaus School, they were celebrating their centenary year. They were to give the teachers a big party and take them on a picnic. I was invited to join the celebrations as a lead up to the final day. I knew that it wasn't appropriate for a recently widowed woman to be seen celebrating in public – "What would people say?" was the 1st question my mum thought of asking when I told her about it. It wasn't done! Widows were meant to wear colours of mourning like black or grey. I thought about it and felt torn.

I knew deep inside that it would do me a world of good to be part of the festivities.

Rony would never have wanted me to mope around or continue to be sullen and reclusive. He always preferred that I lived joyously and celebrated life just as he had done – He truly lived for the moment and appreciated everyone around him, building them up in such a positive way! No one left his company without feeling happier, lighter or special. He had a unique way of uplifting people he came in contact with. He'd see the funny side of things and his light-heartedness was contagious.

I decided that as long as I'm doing something that will bring me happiness, that is not scandalous or displeasing in God's sight, I had nothing to worry about! I didn't have to answer to society but only to Him. I gave in my name to attend the celebrations. I wore a beautiful blue dress to the gala event, which we enjoyed very much. The teachers were delighted that I'd decided to come and to those who thought differently, I wasn't going to lose sleep over it. What they thought or said was none of my business and it was also out of my control so no point in my stressing over it.

What a great time I had! We were each given a gold pendant – A small Grape Vine – an intricate memento. I was glad about my bold choice and I felt Rony patting me on my back for being myself and not letting societal norms get in the way of my having a well-deserved good time.

You need to persevere, for when you have done the will of God, you will receive what he has promised. – Hebrews 10:36

Chapter 15

Silver Linings Playback

Looking back at these 29 years, I thank God for gracing me with the desire to follow His will and for the peace of mind, only *He* can bring!

Another blessing that came into my life soon after Rony's passing, was that I was asked to go for a recollection to Goregaon seminary with the Widows Movement. I recall doubting whether it was a good idea as all the other widows were much older than me, every one of them a grandmother. I thought to myself, "What am I doing here?" But my instincts were wrong; what a wonderfully enlightening experience it was for me!

The women shared about their lives; how they had also lost their husbands many years before and how God looked after each one of them and their children, who were now abroad, doing so well, with children of their own. I said to the Lord, "If you've looked after these faithful women; these widows, your promise for the orphans and the widows is true for me too!" It built my faith and trust even more, that he would see to the needs of my children and settle them well.

Soon after that, a few months later, I was asked to join the Fraternity of Our Lady of the Resurrection (F.O.L.O.R). This was a group formed in France by widows for widows. The group was formed in 1943, where a group of Widows of WWII came together to consecrate themselves to Christ and to give their time and dedication to the movement to offer hope and uplift widows across the world.

Many men lost their lives during the war and left behind young widows. It was a silent mission to offer our widowed lives for married couples, priests and for fellow widows. The F.O.L.O.R is composed of 14 regions all over the world. This mission which is always full of 'hope and life' (from the Lord), requires the Fraternity Family to be constantly inspired with love and communion for each other as well as for the Lord. The Fraternity shares in a universal widowhood where widows globally are made aware of their belonging to a beautiful community of sisters that reaches beyond all borders, experiencing the peace and joy of Jesus and Mary. Each of us members pray that the Lord and His Mother (patroness of widows), bless and uplift every widow. It is a calling and a vocation.

I was wondering how I would manage with young kids, but when you trust God, he takes care of everything. I felt very grateful to have the support of my mum – She was someone I could rely on. She was such a big help in those years when the children were in school and college. Later on she began to forget things with the onset of Alzheimer's and would get confused and feel blank and lost. She clung to her rosary and would recite her prayers faithfully. She also suffered from incontinence due to old age. It was tough to handle. Those were difficult times, trying our best to be patient and caring. Eric and Josephine looked after her during this time and did everything they could. It wasn't easy. She eventually passed away peacefully, in her sleep, one day before her 90th birthday in January 2007. May her soul rest in peace.

I believe that after I joined the fraternity, the biggest change was the commitment that I made which kept me close to the Lord – the commitment of my prayer time, surrendering my day to the Lord, reading the word, going to the Eucharist daily, attending recollections and retreats, which were all so important as we need those breaks. We need to get in touch with our inner selves, to feel the love and tenderness of the Lord, to refuel, rejuvenate and come back refreshed to our everyday routines. This resultant connection with God became an integral part-and-parcel of my routine and I have received many special blessings for this direct and on-going connection with Him.

The first few years of married life, as I mentioned, we were like nomads and I'd had the opportunity to visit so many countries and places abroad. We used to come back to Bombay for holidays. After Rony passed away, I didn't expect to ever be able to go abroad again; I thought it was the end of my trips to a foreign land. I wouldn't be able to afford it for one and with the children, it would be virtually impossible. But God can never be out beaten in His generosity; he had exciting plans for me.

I was nominated and sent by the F.O.L.O.R in 1993, to attend the jubilee year (50 years) of the movement. My brother being in the airlines, I got a free 'subject to load' ticket to France on Air India. Everything was to be taken care of by the fraternity when we arrived there – our stay, our food and I would even get the opportunity to visit our Lady of Lourdes. I realised, as I was sitting in that plane over to France, contemplating God's blessings and giving thanksgiving for His gifts, that it was the 20th of July, Rony's Birthday and that he would have been 50 years too that day! What are the 50-50 chances! Another sweet 'coincidence' to affirm both God's Love and my number one to intercede on my behalf; my husband Rony, who I believed was doing much more for me than would have been possible in his human form. The whole experience was remarkable. The F.O.L.O.R celebration was so well organised and Lourdes was surreal.

On our way back, at the airport, I was informed that Air-India was on strike. They had no idea how long it would last. It was an indefinite strike. They accommodated all the Air-India passengers to the next British Airways flight via London to Delhi. The next blow I received was when they informed me that I could not be accommodated as my ticket was a staff ticket and it was after all 'subject to load'.

They said I would have to wait for the next Air-India flight and they were not sure when the airline strike was going to be called off – It could be a few days, a week or even a month. I was numb. I didn't know what to do! My travel companions, the Widows from the F.O.L.O.R, were off to the U.K on their respective flights; they booked via London so they could stay with their relatives on the way back. I had absolutely no company, no one to stay with and hardly any money in my pockets; I didn't anticipate I would need much, as it was an all-expenses-paid trip.

I began to feel weak in the knees. All I wanted to do was to get home.

I didn't know who to turn to or what to do? The airline staff suggested that I go back to where I came from in France itself and wait it out till they knew more about the strike situation. I began to storm heaven and I told God that I was His responsibility and He had to look after me somehow. There was a kind staff member who saw my plight and told me he would help show me where the rest rooms were, where I could spend the night. He promised to get me something to eat as well. Already I could see God's hand beginning to work; angels were being sent my way.

The kind gentleman suddenly came up to me and suggested that I request British Airways to give me a seat. I told him I was on a 'subject to load' staff ticket and he smiled in resignation. "Then it's virtually impossible! They won't be able to do anything." I felt that God was nudging me to try. So I rationalised that I have nothing to lose! I went up, much against my will, to request them. I asked the Lord to lead me to the right staff member who would be willing to listen. One of the three ladies at the counter looked up and I took that as a sign and approached her. She listened patiently. I began to have hope as she was actually giving me the time of day! However, after I said my piece, she just smiled and shrugged her shoulders, "I'm so sorry ma'am! It's impossible! We are already full up and even if we weren't we don't take staff ticket passengers!" I thanked her gratefully for listening and moved away from the counter.

I felt lost. But I expected that reaction. I continued to pray and believe that God would work His wonders yet. I just kept praising His glorious name over and over again and I clung to my belief that He was going to take care of everything!

Suddenly, I saw the lady at the counter, look at me and she began talking animatedly to her colleague, her senior officer. He also looked in my direction and I could make out by the body language that they were both discussing my case. The man looked disgruntled and very busy as he had a huge line of passengers waiting to be attended to. He just waived off his hand dismissively and I could hear him scolding her for even asking. She too shrugged and went back to her work.

I prayed for the kind lady who attempted to speak to him on my behalf and I asked God to bless her for putting herself on the chopping block like that for the sake of a stranger. Her kind gesture was touching. I even prayed for the hassled officer that he may cool down.

Once again my hope began to diminish, when suddenly, the officer after having walked away in a huff, returned and strode up to me, from nowhere and demanded my passport! I was shocked and pleasantly so! I handed it over to him obediently and ran after him like a helpless puppy wagging its tail; hope, now filling my being!

He went over to the counter and asked them to endorse my ticket. We went to the check-in line and I was asked to stand there and wait my turn. I thanked him for being an angel. They were indeed used by God and had been implanted with the thought to help me out.

There were three passengers ahead of me. Suddenly, the officer in charge at my counter announced that she was going for her lunch break and that she would not be taking more passengers. "Please re-direct the passengers to the next counter." The ground staff there came up to us and stopped next to me.

She re-directed everyone behind me to the next counter and they had to start over behind many others. Life was unfair sometimes but not to me it seemed. God was on my side and no one could get in my way! I praised His name for looking after every small detail at every stage.

When I got to the counter, the lady looked at my papers and my passport and looked up at me with an apologetic expression. "I'm sorry ma'am! But I'm afraid you will not be able to board this plane as you do not have a transit visa for the U.K and the plane is scheduled to stop over in London on its way to Delhi. "But I'm not going to leave the airport. I don't want to stay there even for a minute!" I said. I just want to get straight back to India. "Even so, Ma'am! All transiting passengers need a transit visa irrespective of whether they leave the airport or not. You will be fined a hefty sum of money if you don't have one. We cannot put you on the flight! So sorry!"

The Lord was testing my faith. My heart sank for the third time, I felt weak in the knees and I cried out to him to come to my rescue as he had done several times in the last few hours. I continued to believe that he would not leave me stranded. I had been so delighted and now I was so dejected. "Why? Lord! Why is this happening?"

"Looks like your prayers are all being answered by Mama Mary of Lourdes." said the staff member who had helped me earlier, thinking I was on my way home. I told him that I'd visited the shrine. "There goes my breakfast tomorrow morning!" I thought. I felt all-alone and self pity began to well up, when I remembered the passage from the bible, Thessalonians 1:5 saying, *"In everything give thanks."* I kept surrendering and thanking him over and over again even though I felt abandoned.

Suddenly, the same lady, who'd spoken to her senior earlier, saw me looking very disappointed, came up to me and took my passport, although she had already packed up to go home. She disappeared with it for over forty-five minutes and I must admit how negative thoughts began to disturb my hopeful positivity. "Where has she gone? I don't even know her name! What if she doesn't return with my passport?! What would I do?" I had to consciously throw out every semblance of negativity from my brain and I waited patiently, still clinging on to the belief that God was working in and through her to get me on that flight back home.

Almost an hour later she returned with my passport and my boarding pass. "Mrs. Pereira! Here is your boarding pass. I have spoken to a colleague in London airport. Here are his contact details. He will wait for you at this counter when you transit and he will take care of you and make sure you get back on the flight that will leave for Delhi. Wish you a safe flight. You can relax now." I couldn't thank her enough for what she had done. I said, "Bless you and your whole family! You are God's angel for spending so much time just for me." She was beaming and glowing and the kindness she had shown was marvellous. How I praised God for working through her!

I couldn't believe it when I actually made it on the flight, was seated in my seat and the flight was getting ready to take off on the runway. I felt the tension release. The stress dissipated. The airhostess asked if I wanted something to drink and I boldly requested for a 'Bacardi and coke' I treated myself to something stiff and strong! I raised my glass to heaven and said in my mind, "Cheers! You are my King and I am your princess!" I felt His pampering and I truly felt like royalty. I praised God as we took off. I felt His wind beneath my wings that night.

When we reached Delhi, I enquired about the Air-India flights. They were still on strike. I asked if I could get onto another code share flight instead, but they said I would have to pay full fare. I spoke to my brother Eric and he advised me to stay the night in Delhi, as the strike was likely to be called off soon. I asked for a place to stay for the night – the rates in comparison were a pittance to what had been quoted in France. I happily paid the amount in Indian rupees and was on my way over to see the rooms with the porter, who was helping me with my bag, when I stopped to make a call home.

Noella picked up the line and when she said, "Mummy! Is that you?" with such joy in her voice, I just broke down like a little baby. I cried my eyes out and sobbed with mixed feelings really. It was pent up emotions pouring all out. "Noella! It's so good to hear your voice." I burst out! She was immediately concerned and kept asking if everything was ok. I assured her I was fine and that I was actually so happy to hear her voice. I explained to her briefly about my ordeal in France, so she knew I was headed home soon.

My face always got swollen, even if I cried for a few seconds. My nose was all red and my eyes were still teary. But how relieved I felt to be so close to home! Only one leg left. It would soon be over. The porter had seen me break down on the phone. He thought I had received some bad news from home. Very tentatively he enquired in Hindi, "Kya Hua Madam!" (What happened Madam?) "Sab kuch teekh hain? (Is everything all right?) Aapka Devar kidhar hein? (Where is your husband?), he asked, looking very concerned. I blurted out, "Pati murr gaya!" (My husband died.) My Hindi wasn't very good to add to the confusion and he looked aghast. He presumed I had just got the news and that's why I was such a sorry mess. "Aaaaah! Maaf karna Madam!" (Aaaah! Sorry Madam!) He felt so bad. He was immediately filled with compassion and went off to get me a cup of tea and a snack to eat. His love and concern was another amusing way God showed His love, yet again, through this simple and sweet angel.

It was another reason to laugh at how God works in mysterious and sometimes amusing ways.

The next morning, I found out that there was a plane coming into the Delhi airport and leaving for Bombay, but it was only refuelling and would not take any new passengers because of security reasons. It was scheduled to come in at 12 noon and would leave by 12:30 pm. I was hopeful, but the officers said not to raise my hopes, as they would not be opening the flight at all.

I was still waiting for my baggage from British airways, which hadn't come in the previous night on my flight in. All the bags had come in and the very last to arrive were my bags. As soon as I saw them, I grabbed hold of it and rushed towards the Air India counter to see if I could convince them to get me on the flight. "We're very sorry madam! But the flight is already on the runway." I glanced at the clock. It was already 12:15 pm.

I cried out like a little child, pleading with the officers. "Please bring the plane back! It can't go without me! It came here to take me and it can't leave me behind!" They all looked at me pitiably, probably thinking I had lost my mind. I cried to the Lord yet again! "You have brought me this far and you have sent this plane for me! I know it! Only you can bring it back to take me!"

"Great is the Lord and happy is he with the humble of heart who trust in His will." The impossible was made possible yet again! The officers received news that the Air-India flight had had some technical problem and was returning from the runway. When I heard them discussing this, I literally yelled out, "It's come back for me!" They tried to calm me down and explained that the plane hadn't been opened at all. They would merely sort out the problem and it would be on its way again.

I prayed and believed and was convinced that the plane was delayed because of me. What was to follow was one of the most wondrous miracles I had ever experienced!

Two whole hours after the technical problem was rectified, they were forced to open the flight as two passengers, a husband and his wife had insisted on getting off the aircraft, for fear that the plane might crash.

"Praise you, Jesus!" I shouted. "Would you like to take their place, Madam?" The officers inquired. They knew it was a rhetorical question. Of course, I wanted to! It had come back and was opened only for Mrs. Mildred Pereira! 15 minutes later, I was on my way back home to Bombay on a flight that had been specially directed into Delhi, exclusively to pick me up and take me home to my family. I was indeed the Lord's Princess as the Royal treatment just kept getting better and better!

I say so because the story doesn't end there! When I got to Bombay airport safe and sound, my brother was there to greet me and he was taking my bags out to the taxi when he bumped into a friend of his, who had come to pick up his relatives and he had missed them somehow.

Eric knew he stayed in Bandra so he asked, "Hey! Are you headed home or going somewhere else after this?" His friend offered to give me a lift. "I'm going to Bandra. Would you like a lift home?" He said. "I'm going back empty." I looked at Eric and he answered for me. "That will be great!" So we got into his posh and spacious air-conditioned car and were reached right to the doorstep in style. I looked up towards heaven and winked. "You are tremendous in your pampering Lord!" He looked after me every step of the way and I am so happy to give this testimony to so many over and over again, reliving God's miracles in my life so that others may hear and believe the good news. He is our loving Father and he wants the best for us always and at every juncture and though sometimes it may not be so evident immediately, if we cling on to His promise, we will see His light and find our way every single time.

"Come to me all ye who labour and I will give you the peace and rest that you deserve!" Alleluia! *And not only this, but we also exult in our tribulations, knowing that tribulation brings about perseverance; and perseverance, proven character; and proven character, hope; - Romans 5:3-4*

Chapter 16

The Protector Of The Widow

On the 20th of February 2015, I completed a landmark; 70 years on God's fine planet. When I look at my children today all settled, married off to fantastic spouses of their own, with children of their own, I can't help marvel at the incredible circle of life. It reminds me of the touching song from one of my favourite classic movies, "Fiddler On the roof!" It went like this....

"Sunrise, Sunset, Sunrise Sunset, swiftly flew the years! Is this the little girl I carried? Is this the little boy at play? I don't remember growing older, When did they? When did she get to be a beauty? When did he grow to be so tall? Wasn't it yesterday when they were small? Sunrise, Sunset, Sunrise, Sunset, swiftly flow the days. Seedlings turn overnight to sunflowers, Blossoming even as we gaze. Sunrise, Sunset, Sunrise, Sunset, swiftly fly the years, One season following another, Laden with happiness and tears. What words of wisdom can I give them? How can I help to ease their way? Now they must learn from one another, Day by day. They look so natural together. Just like two newlyweds should be. Is there a canopy in store for me? ☺ Sunrise, Sunset, Sunrise, Sunset, swiftly fly the years. One season following another, Laden with happiness, And Tears.

This beautiful song never fails to bring a tear of joy to my eye. It encompasses so beautifully, how we move so swiftly from one phase to another, learning and evolving each day. God chisels us like a diamond stone craft, smoothening away rough edges, bringing out the beauty of our inner glow and every nuance of our unique personalities, so we may touch each other in our own little or large circle of influence.

Every one of us is like an instrument, just waiting to be played so that the melody might uplift another but God waits patiently for us to tune it so he can play his masterpiece through us.

Over the years, the kids worked hard. They studied hard, did well in their respective fields and each secured good jobs.

Roslynn's wedding on July 27th 2013, in the Raddison Blu, South Goa with the entire family.

They are all settled and each pursuing their passions and using their God given talents, which gives me great joy!

Albert is an entrepreneur and businessman and runs a digital advertising firm of his own. He's married to Preeti and they have two girls Gia and Jade.

Noella is an Author and Voice Artiste married to Satish, a devout Hindu who is so Christ-like in his approach to life. I was honoured to be the guest of honour at her book launch in Singapore.

Roslynn is a theatre actress, compere and event host. She also runs her own YouTube channel playing quirky characters like 'Aunty Maggy' and 'Milly' – who she named after me.

She got married to Rocky, a Sindhi businessman in July 2013. She'd so wanted to fulfil my wish that at least one of my children would marry someone within the Christian faith.

It was tough to accept. Each time they came to me, with the news that they were serious about someone, I hoped and prayed that they would find good Christian spouses but the Lord continues to teach me to open my mind and to accept that many religious practices and rituals are manmade and that he loves all human beings as His children. It's not easy to let go of our baggage and our indoctrination. It becomes part of our psyche. So each time, for all my three children, I had to die to desires. He reminds me that once I surrender, he will do the rest for the best.

It's always a tough battle for us parents to allow our children to walk down their own path, allowing them to fall and make their share of mistakes. Sometimes, we see them taking a wrong turn and it is our instinct to protect, to shelter and to guide them to the right path so we can save them from the pitfalls along the way but it is their unique growth curve. We need to step aside and allow it to take form, even at the cost of the graph tipping and diving at times.

Jesus, our loving father does the same with each of us. He allows us our free will and steps in when we cry out to him to take over. Jesus looked after them.

After my husband's passing, I'd often feel bad for my children; that I couldn't afford to give them the best of everything like their father would have done if he were alive. They were deprived of the trendy clothes, the gadgets, the holidays and the outings. All the fun just came to a standstill. I'd feel inadequate because I wasn't as good a cook like my sisters-in-law, I wasn't as creative or knowledgeable as my neighbours and I wasn't as good at organising outings. I felt guilty that I didn't push my children more to excel, have the money to enrol them in expensive extra curricular activities or spend on toys or birthdays & Christmas parties for them. But I realised that as they got older, their best memories were of the times I came to their school to deliver their hot home cooked lunch and they got to see me during school hours or how I'd help them learn songs I knew for their singing competitions or pick out a piece for their elocution or how they couldn't wait to get home to tell me when something important happened in their lives. They felt free to vent, to rant and let out steam and that if I happened to step out when they came home, they were so disappointed but would be soothed with the love notes I'd leave for them on the door. I was relieved to realise that my children remembered the love and the attention more than the stuff they were given or not given.

Roslynn was to marry Rocky on the 3rd of January 2013 but on the 21st of December 2012, at her bachelorette party, she was playing a game the girls had organised and being the competitive person she is, she went all out to win! Unfortunately, she slipped in the stockings she was wearing and twisted her ankle. At first she thought that is was just a sprain but when they took an x-ray, they found that it was a fracture and that she would have to be in a cast for two months. The irony was that Rocky's bachelor party was a skydiving adventure party; talk about who went out and broke a leg!

She was so disappointed with the news. She didn't want to get married in a cast on a wheelchair. She had been planning her wedding and had dreamt about the day for as long as I could remember. This was perhaps their first test as a couple. Despite the fact that everything had been booked, the invites were sent, the events were planned, the dress was made; they postponed the wedding indefinitely. Rocky wanted to give her the wedding of her dreams and he reached the decision that it was better to postpone than go through with a half-baked one that made everyone else happy except them. Roslynn was relieved that he supported her and she grew closer and respected him even more for it.

Rony had always said that Roslynn would be the one who would be there with me for a long time, keeping me young and his prediction came true; this situation compelled her to be housebound. It was a bonus time I got with her, all to myself. I was able to share with her all I wanted to about marriage, about giving, about respect and trust. We grew closer than ever. She needed that extra time to get over her fears of the unknown and our prayers together helped her feel even more assured. I see a lot of Rony in Roslynn; that same larger than life spirit and humour. She was so little when he passed away and though he wasn't around to influence her, he had made his impact and his essence lives on in her. He would have been proud of the woman she's turned out to be today.

God has a plan for everything including misfortunes. I was happy that she took this in her stride and imbibed my faith. I'm sure the breaking of her leg was a small price to pay for the nurturing of her soul!

Seven months down the line On July 26th and July 27th they said their "I do's" in front of their friends and family in Goa's posh Radisson Blu... and Boy! Was it worth the wait!! It was a destination wedding fit for a Prince and Princess! - A GRAND wedding after her own heart. Fr. Errol said the mass on Roslynn's request and he very sweetly flew down to Goa for the wedding. He gave a meaningful, thought-provoking sermon on religious integration, patience, love and service and touched the hearts of the many people of other faiths that were present in the congregation. He said, "Rocky calls God by a different name and Roslynn calls God by a different name but He has only one name and that is LOVE."

If we but touch and make a difference to even one person who comes our way, our life will have had a meaningful purpose. Life in itself is a gift and such a blessing! I am truly grateful for waking up each morning and being able to take a deep breath. I hope and pray that each of my children and their children and their children's children may trust and believe in the good Lord, like I have done; that they may dedicate their lives to His greater glory and that they may read His word like fodder for their souls and hear His voice in all things small and big, then I can pass on, in peace, knowing that my work here on earth is done. When you teach your sons and daughters to trust the Lord, you teach their sons and daughters too and the whole clan shall follow His word and give Him praise and I can triumphantly proclaim that all mine shall be in His favour.

Growing old is imperative and our passing on is an inevitability of being human. I try to remind myself to live each day in communion with the Lord, as if it were my last. It helps me value my relationships a whole lot more, prioritize people over things and helps me serve and love others with the importance they deserve.

God continues to show me His little signs, work tiny miracles and big miracles in my life on an on-going basis; He reminds me each time that He cares, He loves me and He loves mine.

My grandchildren, Gia, Jade, Ved and Ronav bring such joy and laughter to me. They are being brought up in good, loving homes and I'm proud of each one of them; each blessed with their own set of talents and personalities to brighten up my days. They are so affectionate and their innocence never fails to amuse me.

Preeti is a dependable daughter-in-law and such a multi-tasker! She is friendly and warm and the girls rely on her. She's a huge help to Albert, in running his start-ups.

In 2014, she told Albert, one day, that she had been contemplating a decision ever since Roslynn's wedding, the previous year – She felt in her heart that she wanted to become a Christian. Albert had never once requested, suggested or even remotely pointed her in that direction at all and neither did I. We all respected her background and her beliefs. So it came as a big but very pleasant surprise.

When you hear, "We have some good news! Can you guess what it is??" It sounds like an announcement of another baby on the way but when I found out, I realised there *was* a baby on the way indeed! Another baby leaps into Christ's loving arms. If, more than the formality of the procedure or the significance of the ritual, she is able to truly depend on the Lord for all her needs, I will know she and her family are in the best hands ever!

Psalm 68:5 – "Father of the fatherless and protector of widows is God in His holy habitation."

Chapter 17

The Merry Tongue…

On the 20th of February, 2005 I was asked to join Noella and family in their home on Mount Mary's Road, a few buildings down the road from my own home, for dinner with Eric, Jo and family. I remember wearing a black blouse and how Preeti, my daughter in law, kept insisting I change it, as it was looking so drab. I recall how I didn't want to as I was only going to Noella's home and didn't understand why she was making a big deal of it.

I wore the blouse anyway, much to her disappointment and as we arrived at the 'Le Papillon' entrance and I began to walk down the sloping car path, again Preeti insisted we take the footpath instead. When she and I walked next to the garden lawns, suddenly the lights came on and over 75 people shouted in unison…
SUUURRRRRPRISE!!!"

I was simply astounded! Loud drum rolls and music began playing in the background. I had absolutely no idea that the children had arranged a surprise birthday party for me, behind my back and had invited all my friends, relatives, school teachers, prayer group members, priests; even Bishop Bosco was there!!

The surprises kept coming! Albert & Roslynn had put together a video, which they played on a BIG white screen with a projector. It was a tribute to my life gone by with beautiful videos and stills from the past; footage we had on the bridge of 'Hanciet', sandy escapades on the beach, Albert and Noella dancing on the deck with their dad at age 3 and 5 years of age and footage of me when I was still in my early thirties. It was followed by wishes from everyone across the world, messages from Rony's brother from the U.K, my sister-in-law, my nephews, my school principal, my students, from Josephine and Eric and my mum, tributes from my children; the surprises just rolled, one after the other and it was simply overwhelming! A flood of emotions swept over me. I couldn't believe they'd actually done all this and that too managed to keep it a complete secret. I hadn't suspected anything at all!

I kept looking around and was surprised to see each one – thinking to myself, "Oh! She's also here and he's here too!!" Everyone kept coming up to wish me and it was such a fabulous feeling.

The children sang me a beautiful song to the tune of 'Hero' by Mariah Carrey. Noella penned those verses and they'd recorded the song in a professional studio, with all their voices singing each verse. It was so touching and made me feel so blessed. It felt good to be loved.

"You're our Hero! Mom, you've made us what we are! All these years you've been our strength, our hope our joy! You're our idol! With a soul that's loved by God! And the wisdom that you had has been our guide!

Chorus: You're our Hero mum, you are! You gave us strength to carry on! And you cast our fears aside and we knew we could survive! So when we felt like hope was gone! We looked to you and you were strong! Then we learnt to face the truth! That our Hero lies in you!

It's been a long road, when you faced the world alone. Jesus reached out His hand for you to hold.

And you found His love when you searched within yourself. And the emptiness you felt just disappeared.

Lord knows! Our dreams were hard to follow, but you didn't let anyone tear them away! But we held on, coz there would be tomorrow and in time we found 'The Way'

My 60th year certainly started with a bang! They catered a lavish spread and the tables were all decorated with balloons. I was elated! It is a day I will cherish for the rest of my days!

God expressed and showed me His love in various ways from the time I was born till today, giving me a peace that no one else can give, only he; certainly not the world. John 3:16 says, *"God so loved the world that He gave His only son, that whosoever believes in Him, will have eternal life!"* In and through Jesus' death and resurrection, he has given us the strength, power and grace through the Holy Spirit to overcome our obstacles, doubts, fears, anxieties, and illnesses, whatever they might be.

I have experienced this now more so than ever before. When I was growing up I knew about Jesus, about His gospel, about His word and that childhood inculcation from faithful parents, who would always depend on *Him*, held me in good stead. The transition however, though gradual, was imminent; from a God-fearing devout, pious Christian girl, following the directives and the norms of the Church, for FEAR of God's wrath, to a God-loving woman of true faith, relying on God's word and His magnificent, all encompassing LOVE.

Philippians 4:13 says, *I can do all things in Christ who strengthens me.* I believed in those words wholeheartedly! My whole life has been a living testament to His great power and glory. I used to feel that miracles were a thing of the past and happened only during His lifetime or in the old testament of the Bible, but it's not true. He works His wonders and miracles even today! Philippians 4:19 says, *My God will supply all my needs according to His riches and glory!* I've seen this happen in my life. Every single need, want, and desire he sees to. Sometimes we may not even have planned something or consciously wanted something ourselves but he plans it for us and we are left astounded at how much for the best it is! He saw to every last detail; my job and career, my children, my relatives, my friends, my spiritual evolution, my home, my health and even something I always had no idea about; my finances.

When I was ill, I'd have friends come over and help out with a delicious dish or when I needed money, exactly how much I needed would come unto me. When I was low, he'd send someone to boost my morale, I'd read a passage that would speak to me directly and I'd feel better almost instantaneously! He is omnipresent, omnipotent and His love is boundless. He is my spouse, my father, my brother, and my most intimate confidante.

Life wasn't always smooth sailing; It isn't meant to be in this human realm. There are always ups and downs in everyone's lives. It's how we choose to face these challenges and pass these tests that add to our brownie points on our 'eternal bliss' record. The cliché is true – 'What doesn't kill you makes you stronger.'

Six months after Rony's passing, I realised that there were two lumps in my breast. They had turned hard and were beginning to hurt while I bathed or changed. I immediately had a biopsy done.

No doubt fears, that weren't from the Lord, crept in. "What if it was cancerous? What if I had to go through chemotherapy? What if I died of cancer and my children were left orphans?"

Negativity has an insidious nature. Once you allow your mind to dwell on these thoughts, they creep in like a powerful snake and bare their venomous fangs, creating chaos and a flurry of emotions you seem to have less and less control over.

The minute these thoughts would occur, I would drive them out in the name of Jesus! I would hand over the whole situation to him and ask him to take over. I would practice the art of surrender. "You know best Lord! I trust that you will do the best for me and my children." As soon as you surrender, you feel His peace. The whole load and tension of coping is released and you no longer feel helpless. Ironically, in our helplessness and humility and in dying to ourselves, we feel more in control and are truly alive!

The biopsy results I received showed that the lumps were both benign. I'd detected them in time and the doctor advised that I have them removed to be on the safer side. I went in for the operation to have the lumps lanced out. Luckily they were not too deep and the operation was a success. The lumps were gone but I had two scars next to my cleavage, to remind me of God's mercy.

God used me in various ways to bring comfort to people that needed a listening ear. The discernment I received from God spoke through me. I was made a Eucharistic Minister. As part of our responsibilities, we were to go over to give Holy Communion to those who couldn't make it to church due to a chronic illness or immobility.

I had a list of a few residences. I'd go every week. I'd pray with them, talk to them; a visit they all begun to look forward to. I felt I was adding value to their lives by bringing them Jesus through the host, reading the Bible to them or simply paying them a patient listening ear. I knew how important it was to them, so I tried to make sure not to miss the appointment.

When I woke up one morning, as usual, I dedicated my day to the Lord and asked him to use me, as an instrument to do His will. Later that day, I got a call from my neighbour's friend, requesting me to come over to say a thanksgiving prayer at her mum's memorial service. She said that the *Pundit* or Priest she had organised wasn't able to make it at the last moment and she suddenly thought of me.

She was a Hindu lady so she made sure to assure me that it was ok to say the prayers in any way I felt comfortable. I wasn't too sure about their customs and traditions and I also didn't know her well at all. I made up some excuse that I was busy and declined her invitation. However, when I reflected on it, I felt I must call her back and accept. She had, after all, reached out to me and I was free that day – I'd asked God to use me to do his will just that very morning – How could I refuse.

The day arrived and I'd prepared a few verses from the Bible, which I felt were comforting. When I went over, I saw that the whole place was packed with people. I prayed that God would put the words in my mouth and would speak through me, of His message to these people in mourning. I opened my mouth to pray and the words just spilled out of me. I said 'The Lord's Prayer' and reflected on each line in context for the people present.

I thanked God for the gift of their mother, I asked for a healing for those family members who grieved and were missing her and I read out appropriate verses from the Bible about healing and surrender. I read The Beatitudes….

> *"Blessed are the poor in spirit,*
> *for theirs is the kingdom of heaven.*
>
> *Blessed are they who mourn,*
> *for they shall be comforted.*
> *Blessed are the meek,*
> *for they shall inherit the earth.*
>
> *Blessed are they who hunger and thirst for righteousness,*
> *for they shall be satisfied.*
>
> *Blessed are the merciful,*
> *for they shall obtain mercy.*
>
> *Blessed are the pure of heart,*
> *for they shall see God.*
>
> *Blessed are the peacemakers,*
> *for they shall be called children of God.*
>
> *Blessed are they who are persecuted for the sake of righteousness,*
> *for theirs is the kingdom of heaven."*
>
> *Gospel of St. Matthew 5:3-10*

The lady was ever so grateful that I'd agreed to come and thanked me profusely. The family were also very warm and said how meaningful and touching the prayer service was!

I don't know how God put it in the mind of the lady to call me and in what way the Holy Spirit used me to reach out to those faithful people that day, but the lesson he taught me was to follow His will. I learnt to leave myself open to His calling, irrespective of my own reservations, comfort zones, pre-conceived notions and to keep an open mind – All religions were for the good of mankind and he loves each one of His creations – He was teaching me, slowly but surely, true acceptance, love and service to all!

I recall another marvellous incident of how I'd gone over to pray with my friend's mother, who was ill and was in the hospital.

It was an open ward and there was another patient in the next bed. She was to be discharged the very next day, as she was fit and fine. She told me that the lady I had come to see was taken in for some tests and that it would take a while before she returned to her room. So I thanked her and left to go for mass. However, on the way down, I felt the urge to go back and talk to the lady in the next cubicle, who was alone and seemed like she needed the company. I felt the Lord directing me.

She was so happy that I'd returned. We struck up a conversation and she began telling me that she was nervous to go home, as there was tension in her household. She lived with her son and his family and she felt that her daughter-in-law wasn't going to be happy to receive her back. The couple often fought with each other and she felt that she was the cause of their squabbles quite often.

I listened and allowed her to spill her anxieties out. Then I suggested we pray together, for her family and her situation. "Sometimes," I advised, "We feel helpless, as we cannot control our emotions, our circumstances and our relationships. It was best to leave it in the hands of God and to truly surrender."

We said a prayer of repentance for the times she may have said something to hurt her daughter-in-law's feelings, the times she may have acted in haste and intentionally or unintentionally caused rifts within her son's family. We gave those emotions up to the Lord and we asked him to heal each one of her family members, especially her. It was a prayer of thanksgiving and surrender. She had tears in her eyes of relief and of gratitude. I held her hands in mine and reassured her that everything would be fine at home.

Three days later, I went to the hospital again to visit my friend's mother and I enquired about the lady in the next bed, whether her family had come to take her home and if they had heard from her since. I was shocked to hear that she had passed away, the very day of her discharge! She suddenly had a severe stroke and didn't make it. I knew then that God has His ways and He had once again used me to bring His peace and calm to this troubled soul. That prayer of repentance was the pre-healing and surrender she needed to go to her creator's home – one of eternal peace.

After a while, I was elected to be the leader of the Indian Widows group representing the F.O.L.O.R. The following year I went to Paris again. My dream came true as we were also sent to the Holy Land and I got the opportunity to visit Israel, the birthplace of the Lord and the place where he was crucified. It had been a life long desire of mine; the Lord fulfilled this wish as well. It was such an awe-inspiring trip and the feeling of elation to be walking upon the exact spots our Lord had walked, preached, was born in, died upon, was truly a blessing like no other!

Very recently, another desire of mine was fulfilled when I was given the opportunity to visit Fatima, the place where our Lady had appeared to the three children.

I am often called to compere Sports Days in my school, give testimonies and talks, lead prayer meetings, 'Raise the Toast' and 'Say the Grace' at the weddings of my friend's children. I have slowly realised that, though I still feel nervous, the more I put my faith in Him and trust that he will take over my tongue, my thoughts and my actions – he has guided me with the wisdom to make a difference to the lives of many. All I have to do is lean on him like a crutch – and His unrelenting support is, in fact, more like a prosthesis, which props me up, where I know I am too weak to stand on my own.

I find that the butterflies leave my stomach and instead begin to fly forth in the rainbow! I find that my tongue is merry, my heart rejoices in the Lord and my soul is so grateful that I sometimes find myself 'Bursting out of Love' to sing His praises! I love that phrase as my five-year-old grandson, Ronav, expressed it one day so aptly.

As everything keeps falling in place, wrongs become right, sadness flips to joy, weaknesses turn to strengths and as my destiny unfolds and beckons, as I live out each moment in faith, I truly internalise how much he LOVES me and mine and that reassuring knowledge in itself is like touching bliss.

I have had such a fulfilling career at St. Stanislaus School. I joined soon after Rony passed away and though I was to officially retire at age 58 in 2003, I am so grateful to the principal of my school, who asked me to stay on as he felt I had a lot more to offer the boys of St. Stanislaus. He decided to keep me on as a Counsellor for the primary school. The school sent me for a Counsellor's Training through St. Xavier's Institute of Communication.

God showed me how he intended to use a 'Merry Tongue' to bring His good counsel to students, parents and families in need. Sometimes even teachers, who are having a rough day and need a listening ear, come to spend time so that they can pour their hearts out. I pray each time so God's wisdom may flow through me and that I may be used as His channel to broadcast the right advice to his listeners who have tuned in.

Very often, more than even advice, I've noticed people need a listening and empathetic ear with a positive perspective, the healing begins just in getting it off their chests.

I have counselled boys from divorced homes, homes fraught with domestic violence and homes where both parents work and the grandparents are too old to have any control over what goes on. There are students who watch violent TV serials and movies without any adult supervision and it manifests in their behaviour.

Teachers often send me boys from their classes, who they find difficult to deal with. I try to relate to them. I ask them questions that make them open up and I always give them examples they can identify with, usually pertaining to other students their own age or about my own children who went through similar situations. I joke and laugh with them so they begin to feel more at ease and the stigma attached to 'seeing the counsellor' gets removed from their minds.

I try to be as approachable as possible and often go to classrooms to strike up impromptu conversations instead of having them come over to meet me, formerly. I find I am able to get through to the boys when I meet them on their own turf. It's so much less intimidating. My job is so gratifying and it gives me the opportunity to share my first-hand experiences with impressionable minds and make a difference to their lives for the better.

I have flexible hours and go to school thrice a week. This suits me well, given my other commitments to the widows group, prayer and outreach groups, lector responsibilities etc. God keeps me happily busy. I find a good balance and feel fulfilled doing the things I do.

When the children weren't happy in a job or felt like quitting because it was causing them nothing but stress, I went all out to encourage them to do so. I reminded them to focus on their talents and on God's directive rather than the money they would lose out on.

The Lord keeps me merry and my tongue is continually used to wag happily of His greatness. My life and the wondrous testimonies I keep getting opportunities to share is the best possible evangelization I could ever fulfil. It started with my own children at home and though I felt that some of my 'lectures' were falling on deaf ears, they were indeed imbibing more than I imagined they ever would! What greater joy for a parent to have their children demonstrate oodles of gratitude; they never fail to tell me how much they need me, how much they have depended on me and how much they now rely on God themselves.

I recall how, many years before, when I first joined the cell group, Fr. Hillary led our meeting and asked us to close our eyes and imagine Jesus was paying us a visit. He asked us to just feel His presence and let His light shine upon us. We did this for five minutes. He then asked us to reflect on all the blessings in our lives, the talents we were given and the happy events. We were also asked to make a mental note of the negatives and all that we wished we could change. This activity of mindfulness and awareness was an eye-opener for me. I found that I could not think of any talents I possessed but could list many failings very easily. We were to share these out-loud with the rest of our sisters and I felt pretty inadequate and ashamed to not have a single good point to relate. It was also an exercise in humility to share our weaknesses up front.

Fr. Hillary was surprised when I said I had nothing to share as I felt God had forgotten to give me any talents. One of the ladies piped in asking, "So do you think God has made junk?" I boldly answered, "Yes! I guess in my case, he has!" Fr. Hillary just smiled gently. He asked the others present to tell me what they thought of me and they began saying such superlative, kind things. I kept denying these in my mind, thinking they didn't really know the true me and that they'd feel very differently if they only knew me better.

I realised, in hindsight, while sitting before the Blessed Sacrament, in church, how brash and ungrateful I had been. Who was I to ridicule God's creation? I realised, it was my ego talking, an arrogance stemming from my ignorance. I asked for forgiveness that day and I began understanding that while I thought I was humble by admitting I had only faults and weaknesses, it was my pride that ironically kept me from proclaiming my strengths. I learnt that to love and accept myself is the first step on the pyramid of evolution.

On my 70th birthday, my three children got together and decided to throw me another big party. They wanted to invite all my friends and my daughter and family informed me that they would be coming down to India to celebrate the landmark. I was very happy but felt that I would much rather them not spend money unnecessarily, instead, we mutually decided to have a smaller more intimate gathering with just the family.

I planned a smaller get together with refreshments for my various groups: the widows group, the cell group members and my teacher friends, all on separate days leading up to the birthday. My daughters cooked up a sumptuous spread and all my friends were very happy to partake of the meal, wish me and meet the family over a relaxed lunch at home.

On my birthday itself the children whisked me off to Oakwood hotel in Juhu – we checked into posh apartment style rooms with open kitchen and large living room, with 2 bedrooms. We invited my brother Eric to join us – Josephine, was away in the U.S with her daughter who was due to give birth to her first child anytime then.

We had a lovely time. It was relaxing, bonding with the whole family; just the way I liked it.

Just when I thought it couldn't have gotten any better, it did! The kids gifted me a dressy white tunic with lovely embroidered motifs on it and they began an evening of entertainment, starting with my first grandchild, Gia singing her rendition of an apt song, "God gave me you!" She sang so well. Next, all the kids performed a synchronised dance and my two grandsons had come dressed as two little Elvis' with flashy satin attire and the customary sideburns and hair puffs to boot! All my grandkids call me Nana. So a special song just for me was recorded with my daughter's voice. The children danced to "You're all right Nana!" set to the tune of Elvis Presley's 'That's all right Mama!'.

They danced in perfect synchrony and the lyrics were very cute! They went like this....

    Well, You're alright, Nana
    You're alright for sure
    You're alright Nana, just everything bout you!
    Well, you're alright, you're alright.
    You're alright now Nana, everything bout you!

    Nana you're so funny,
    Cute-n-cuddly too
    You just make us laugh,
    And we just love lovin' you!
    Well, you're alright, you're alright.
    You're alright now Nana, everything bout you

    70 years now Nana
    A BIG landmark for sure
    You've shown us how to live and
    We couldn't have asked for more
    Well, you're alright!, you're alright!
    You're alright now Nana, everything bout you!

My granddaughter Jade then did some terrific gymnastics with cartwheels, backflips, handstands and standing bridge. She is so flexible! Then each of the children began reading small written tributes and excerpts that sounded familiar and requested me to unveil what looked like a jewellery box. I unwrapped the cover and there in my hands lay 'The Merry Tongue' – A story of Love, Loss Faith & Surrender – MILLY PEREIRA. I read my own name on the cover of a thick paperback novel. My life story in print. I didn't have a clue they'd planned this surprise....I could hardly believe my eyes! I flipped through the 450+ pages of stories and anecdotes, which was like a quick flashback with photographs from the 'good old days.'

I vaguely recalled that Noella was planning to write a book about my life but that was such a long time ago. The children had outdone themselves. It was THE BEST birthday present I had EVER received.

Our parish organised an inner healing session, which I attended a few months ago. The woman, with the gift of knowledge, who was leading the session, suddenly called out my name. She called out a few others as well. She said, *"Milly!?"* looking around for acknowledgement. I raised my hand. *"God has this message for you. "My ocean of love knows no bounds. You are the SOS vessel. Pray much for what is ahead of you.""*

Holding 'The Merry Tongue' with my name and life story in print. I was overwhelmed and tears of joy fill my eyes. The best birthday gift ever!

I do not know what lies ahead, but I felt God was giving me a confirmation of my faith. He built me up all these years and is now calling me, more than ever to reach out, in faith to my community.

I have learnt, by His gentle guidance, to quietly listen because he talks to us; through Bible verses, through deep reflection, through sharing with our family and through our friends and sometimes through strangers who are used to do or say just the thing we need at that moment or phase in our lives.

I have understood and now believe that there are absolutely no coincidences and that things happen for a reason; we may not perceive how something seemingly bad for us happens but it is permitted to teach us what we need to learn, to cleanse us, to heal us or make us stronger. When something 'Just works out so beautifully!', these signs are God's affirmation and reminders that *His* hand is present at all times and that all we need to do is reach out and hold onto it like a child holds on, with purity of heart and implicit trust.

I have internalised and know that there is indeed a thread of divinity woven into the very fabric of our lives. Life is a blessing and God's Love is eternal; It heals! It is a balm that soothes and converts your sorrow to joy. Not only is your heart unbroken and the ache of loss replaced by peace and acceptance but *His Love* has the power to transform the weakest of us into the strongest and fiercest forces; steadfast, unwavering and springing forth like a fountain – pouring and gushing out so that all who drink from it are refreshed and rejuvenated.

My Faith has and continues to grow, with every experience, with every passing day. *He* shows me that my life of Faith ennobles and enables me to see *Him* in everything, in the trees, the flowers, in the sky, in my own breath, in each other and he rewards my belief, which remains unrelenting, way beyond the power of reason to believe. I believe that he can make the illogical logical and the impossible possible. *"For with God, nothing shall be impossible." Luke 1:37*

The more I surrender my own will to *His*, the more I see His pressed down and overflowing blessings in my life. I claim His promise to be my own, *"Give and it will be given to you; good measure, pressed down, shaken together, running over, they will pour into your lap." Luke 6:38* I'm no longer His doubting Thomas but His Trusting Milly!

I have yet to grow in *His* infinite love. But He loves me despite my failings, my weaknesses and my faults. He embraces me with my imperfections and I feel my greatest purpose, having been made in His likeness, is to do the same to my brothers and sisters while I live on this earth – If in knowing me even one person has known God then my work here will be fulfilled.

God's promises in the Bible are real and made especially for His blessed people who obey *His* will – *"So you have sorrow now; but I will see you again and your hearts will rejoice and no one will take your joy away from you." – John 16:22*

"They that sow in tears shall reap in joy" – Ps. 126:5

For this I am certain: *He* emboldens me, *He* carries me, *He* strengthens me, *He* guides my thoughts and my actions, *He* protects me and mine with His safety blanket. Jesus is my saviour! *"I will never leave you or forsake you." Hebrews 13:5 "For He will give His angels charge of you, to guard you in all your ways." Ps. 91:11*

…Soon after the passing away of my husband, I received a prophecy from God's messenger, Amalia, that I shared right at the very beginning. It had said, *"They will call you to arbitrate in disputes and you will give wise counsel. You will be a healer of breaches where things are in discord. You will be actioned by my spirit. You will say things with a merry tongue; you are not one for graceless words and no one will take offence. I will cause you to instruct many and your words will carry because they are not your words but my words – living words passing from generation to generation even to those yet unborn. I trust you to walk in waterless places and there will be an oasis. Walk where there is no water and there will be flowers to bloom. You will not speak great things but simple things full of life and truth. My daughter Deborah was a prophetess close to my heart. My spirit will breathe into you the prophetic word from the heart of the Lord himself."*

I was intrigued with His beckoning to make me as Deborah was; She was a prophetess, the only woman judge of Israel, in ancient biblical times, around the 12 century BC. She is referred to as a harbinger of peace.

At the time it felt so far-fetched, given my tongue-tied, reserved nature….but I see how that proclamation for me has unfolded so beautifully; How I was called to stay on as a counsellor in my school and more than ever, how my daughter was inspired to write this book so my testimonies might go forth in print for posterity. I see now how I have slowly evolved and emerged just like a butterfly emerges into the light…*"A merry heart doeth good like a medicine, but a broken spirit dries the bones..."* - Proverbs 17:22.

A merry heart maketh a cheerful countenance: but by sorrow of the heart, the spirit is broken. - Proverbs 15:13

"A good tongue is healing; healing to wounded consciences, by comforting them; to sin-sick souls by convincing them; accommodating differences, and reconciling parties at variance." - Proverbs 15:4

"Death and Life are in the power of the tongue, and those who love it will eat its fruits." – Proverbs 18:21

"A Soothing Tongue is a tree of life" – Proverbs 15:4

"Let the words of my mouth and the meditation of my heart be acceptable in thy sight oh Lord! - My strength and my redeemer." – Psalms 19:14

"And my tongue shall speak of thy righteousness and thy praise all the day long!" – Psalms 35:28

I pray now that God may continue to renew me with the Fruits of the Holy Spirit – *love, joy, peace, forbearance, kindness, goodness, faithfulness, gentleness and self-control. Against such things, there is no law.* - Galatians 5:22-23

I often think of Rony and how he must be smiling. He probably watches over me and triumphs in my victories with the good Lord. He is truly the best guardian angel I could ever have!

I remind myself of God's promise - *"Proverbs 3:5,6... "Trust in the LORD with all thine heart; and lean not unto thine own understanding. In all thy ways acknowledge him, and he shall direct thy paths." –* This secret weapon I have passed on to my children too and am delighted to see them take baby steps in faith like I have.

Today, because of God's Great Love, Grace and Mercy, I have found a gradual but sure metamorphosis from the safety of my dark cocoon to a radiant butterfly with wings to fly and acquired colours to radiate – The colours of Faith, Hope, Trust, Surrender and LOVE!

Acknowledgements

I would like to thank Albert, Noella & Roslynn for being such treasures – My gifts from God. Through them, Jesus continues to show me His infinite outpouring of Love.

I owe so much to Rony's family, his brothers, sisters and their families, and to my mum, who sacrificed her personal space and time to help raise my children and to Eric and Josephine without whose support, love and understanding I don't know how I'd have managed.

To Doreen and Ralph whose rock-solid friendship I value deeply and to this day I rely on them for good counsel, a listening ear and their unfailing support.

Fr. Hillary Miranda, may his soul rest in peace, was my first 'Guru', a role model and an example of God's wisdom. I will always hold him dear to my heart.

To Bishop Bosco for his humility and approachability. His taking the time to read, review and write the Foreword for this book, despite his busy schedule is such a blessing! I'm truly honoured and indebted.

Thank you to each and every one of you, who have touched my life with your laughter, your joy and for showing me a semblance of heaven on earth. – Milly

About the Authors

Milly Pereira is a retired school teacher and now serves as a counsellor in a reputed school in Mumbai, India.

She plays an active role in her local church Parish, having served as a Eucharistic Minister and Charismatic Renewal lead for her parish prayer group for many years. She is a member and representative of the (F.O.L.O.R) Fraternity of our Lady of the Resurrection; a widows movement founded in France and has devoted her life to the service of God, trusting in his will for her.

She feels blessed to be used as His instrument to uplift and bring comfort and laughter to the lives of others in her community. She's elated to be able to share her testimonies of Love, Loss, Faith & surrender with the world.

Noella is Milly's daughter in the 'The Merry Tongue' and has been a first-hand witness to most of these experiences and testimonies of faith.

She currently resides in Singapore with her husband and two boys. She says of her experience writing 'The Merry Tongue', "My mum, Milly, is a woman of simplistic faith, filled with the grace of God and her influence in my life has been enormous. She is definitely the 1st God I know – A representation of His love and compassion on earth. She has always exuded an aura of peace. Her gentle uplifting, unwavering belief and constant support have been my guiding force; there wasn't a day when I felt I couldn't come home and find LOVE.

Her empathy and God given wisdom I have deeply admired and if the phrase, 'your children are a reflection of you' holds true, I pray that some day I can look in the mirror and see my mum, because in seeing her... I see divinity. I feel blessed to have been born into her care and her nurturing testimonies of faith, surrender and God's miracles in her life have reaffirmed His all-encompassing unconditional love. My brother, sister and I hope you will benefit from her life journey as we have.

I began writing 'The Merry Tongue' in early 2000 and it was lying unfinished all these years. I rushed to have more than half of it completed within a month, just in time for mum's 70th birthday in 2015, as a surprise gift.

She didn't have a clue what she was made to unveil and it brought tears of joy to her eyes; her testimonies in print. God loves her so and he shows her how much in so many fabulous ways.

Everyone of us has a story to tell. Life offers some unique experiences and some similar ones others can immediately relate to. We share the same planet, the same sky and the same hope, which each of us is intrinsically born with. It is these very essences of the human spirit that link us together far outweighing our differences. Stories and lessons learned, passed on from one generation to the other, are important; They cement the bond of family, leave a rich heritage of legacy for posterity and offer insight and opportunities for contemplation. I do believe that in the age of internet, the more the wealth of these experiences are shared with a wider circle, the richer we collectively become. We grew up with stories that were brought alive in our mind's eye and it gave us our sense of identity, grounded and rooted us, built our self-esteem and connected us to our past like an unseen umbilical cord. I feel privileged to honour my father and mother is this manner and to have been divinely inspired so mum's simple stories of extraordinary faith might reach a wider audience."

Noella is a published author and writer. Her book 'When I Grow Up', was released in 2014. Her script dialogue for 'Haptics' an animated short film produced by the studio she worked for in Mumbai, won top honours at the prestigious Hollywood Film Awards in California. Her articles on women's issues, careers, parenting and relationships have been featured on leading lifestyle & women's magazines like 'The Singapore Women's Weekly', 'India Se', 'Young Parent' and 'Femina' both in Singapore and in India. She is also a professional voice over & jingle artist and runs 'Wonders of the Voice' master classes for aspiring artists. For more information please visit www.voice4ads.com

Glossary

- Dhobi Talao – "Laundryman's Lake" is a neighbourhood in the city of Mumbai (formerly Bombay) in India. Located in the South Mumbai area, it used to be a location where linen was washed. In British times, dhobis or clothes cleaners used to wash the British soldier's clothes here.
- Bazaar – Marketplace
- Konkani – is an Indo-Aryan language belonging to the Indo-European family of languages and is spoken along the western coast of India in the states of Goa, Magalore and Maharashtra.
- Chapatti – Unleavened flat bread made of wheat flour dough eaten widely across India.
- Dowry - an amount of property or money brought by a bride to her husband on their marriage.
- Kanyadhaan - is an Indian ritual in which the father gives away his maiden daughter in marriage to the groom. It is a highly valued marriage ritual. Kanyadaan literally means 'gifting a girl'.
- Zubeda Manzil – Is the name of a building. It has Arabic origins meaning Destination of flowers or the essence of home.
- Complan – Complan Foods makes powdered milk energy drinks, popular in India.
- Balchaon - a Goan speciality pickle made of salted prawns, red chilli, spices and marinated in vinegar.
- Pani Puri – Fried puff-pastry balls filled with spiced mashed potato, spiced water, and tamarind juice. A popular street food of India.
- Bhel-Puri - an Indian dish of puffed rice, onions, spices, and hot chutney.
- Sev puri – is an Indian street food snack and a type of chaat. It is a specialty that originates from Mumbai, Maharashtra.
- Dahi Batata Puri – It is also a street food made of Sev, puri and onion, chilli powder, moong dal, yoghurt and coriander leaves
- Ragda Pattice - is a preparation made from dried white peas and used in chaat items. Ragda means semi-solid pattice.
- The Parsi Dairy farm – is a 100-year-old dairy business in Princess Street, Mumbai that was established in 1916. The dairy produces dairy products and Indian sweets.

- Missal – is a popular dish from Maharashtra, India. It consists of a spicy curry usually made of sprouted moth bean and a type of Indian bread roll. The final dish is topped with potato-chiwda mix, "farsan" or "sev", onions, lemon and coriander (cilantro).
- Lassi – a sweet or savoury Indian drink made from a yoghurt or buttermilk base with water.
- Peda - is a sweet from the Indian subcontinent, usually prepared in thick, semi-soft pieces. The main ingredients are khoa, sugar and traditional flavourings, including cardamom seeds, pistachio nuts and saffron.
- Desi – is a loose term for the people, cultures and products of the Indian subcontinent or South Asia and their diaspora, derived from the Ancient Sanskrit (deśá or deshi), meaning one's land.
- Dufferin – A training ship for cadets or students learning how to be seafarers on a cargo ship.
- Parsi – A member of a group of followers in India of the Iranian prophet Zoroaster. The Parsis, whose name means "Persians", are descended from Persian Zoroastrians who emigrated to India to avoid religious persecution by the Muslims.
- Gymkhana - Recreational centres, community clubs, sports arenas or simply places that facilitate social gatherings originally started by the British in India but still thriving today in main cities.
- Marine Club – Is a seamen's club that provides accommodation, lodging and recreational facilities to seafarers
- Padre – Priest or clergyman.
- Sheng-channa-wallahs – Street vendors that sell roasted gram and peanuts in little conical containers made from old newspaper.
- Tava – Hot cast iron griddle to roast on
- Sukha Bhel' - Dry mixture of puffed dry rice, onions, chutney and spices
- Mirchi-Masala – Chilli-Spice a phrase that is used in 'Hinglish', colloquial language to express adding one's two bit to make a story more interesting and engaging.
- Mutton Xacuti – is a curry prepared in Goa, with complex spices, including white poppy seeds, sliced or grated coconut and large dried red chillies.
- Goan sausage fry - is a typical reflection of Indo-Portuguese cuisine from Goa, Daman and Diu, which once were part of the Portuguese State of India. It is made

with pork, marinated in spices and dried in the sun. It is extremely spicy. Their average diameter is about 1.5 cm.
- Bebinca - also known as bibik or bebinka, is a type of pudding and a traditional Goan dessert. Traditional Bebinca has seven layers. The ingredients include plain flour, sugar, ghee (clarified butter), egg yolk, and coconut milk.
- Aaya – A temporary paid helper experienced in baby and mother oil massage.
- Colaba – A place in South Mumbai where the Taj Hotel or Gateway of India is located.
- Ayurvedic - From the Sanskrit words "ayur," meaning life, and veda," meaning knowledge, referring to ayurvedic medicine.
- Idli – a south Indian steamed cake made of fermented rice and lentils.
- Dosa - in south Indian cooking a pancake made from rice flour and ground pulses, typically served with a spiced vegetable filling.
- Guru – Teacher, Role Model who you look to for guidance.

Bibliography

L. B Cowman, edited by James Reimann. *Streams in the Desert*, 366 Daily Devotional Readings. Excerpts use by permission of Zondervan.

The Holy Bible - Passages & Psalms taken in context to each chapter with a message to contemplate and reflect upon. *Proverbs 24:3-4; Matthew 6:19-21; Jeremiah 29:11; Deuteronomy 32:2; Philippian's 4:13; 1 Corinthians 13:2; Ruth 1:16-17; Peter 3:7; 1 Corinthians 13:4–8a; Matthew 19:4-6; Galatians 5:14; Romans 15:2; Mathew 17:20; Romans 12:2; Mathew 7:9-11; Philippians 4:6-7; Hebrews 10:36; Galatians 2:20; Romans 5:3-4; Psalm 68:5; Luke 1:37; Luke 6:38; Galatians 5:22-23; Proverbs 3:5,6; John 16:22; Ps 126:5; Hebrews 13:5; Ps. 91:11; Proverbs 17:22; Proverbs 15:13; Proverbs 15:4; Proverbs 18:21; Psalms 19:14; Psalms 35:28; Ruth 1:16-17; Peter 3:7; 1 Corinthians 13:4–8a; Gospel of St. Matthew 5:3-10; Thessalonians 1:5; John 3:16; Philippians 4:19*

Lyrics from the hymn taken from the psalm 40:1, 'You gave a song' by Evie Tornquist Karlsson, from the album, 'Unfailing Love' 1981.

Lyrics from the song, 'Sunrise, Sunset' taken from the classic Hollywood musical film, 'Fiddler on the Roof,' Written in 1964 with music by Jerry Bock and text by Sheldon Harnick.

*Note to reader: Some names of people, referred to in the book, have been changed to protect privacy and confidentiality.

www.ingramcontent.com/pod-product-compliance
Lightning Source LLC
Chambersburg PA
CBHW031638040426
42453CB00006B/144